The nth Degree

SIDEREAL TROPICAL: *THEY BOTH WORK*

Rikki Blythe

FISHTAIL ARTS & ASTROLOGY

2022

Dearest Ava and Theo; your mum and dad will roll their eyes and try to tell you Yaiyai is mad believing in astrology; but now you have had a book dedicated to you so they will have to keep at least one copy in your house, hopefully not hidden.

PREFACE

The book, 'Age of the Fishtail' united astronomy with astrology by using the premise that Sidereal and Tropical zodiac systems both work. They do both work.

Fishtail Astrology explores why and how it can be that the Sidereal and Tropical zodiacs both work; because we all know that they do. The formula is a concept which we probably already use, albeit, unconsciously. This book will just make conscious what was already obvious but never much talked about.

The premise of this book is a simple formulaic idea. It is called the nth degree and the nth degree is applied to certain behaviour patterns.

When the characteristic of the Tropical constellation is taken to its nth degree it transmutes into the characteristics of its Sidereal counterpart.

As you read through all the descriptions this concept will make sense of why the Tropical Sun sign can be the same person as the Sidereal Sun sign person. All of the Moon and planetary placements are included too.

The unity of Sidereal and Tropical zodiacs totally satisfies my heart. I feel immense relief in the clarification of this concept and hope that the schism between astrologers will bring new light into astrology as well as dissolving the arrows of our critics.

CONTENTS

FOREWORD

DIAGRAMS

INTRODUCTION

DESCRIPTIONS OF THE 24 DISTINCTIONS

APPENDIX

ASTRONOMY OF PRECESSION OF THE EQUINOXES

WHY FISHTAIL

FOREWORD

This book offers a simple idea, of looking at the 'two zodiacs' in unison. The difference in perspective is a wonder to behold. Rikki Blythe describes the concept of each sign reaching its nth degree; how each sign - Tropical and Sidereal - explains the 'whole person experience'. Along with the Precession of the Equinoxes, Rikki so clearly and succinctly explains the Ages and each of the constellations for both of the zodiacs; I wonder how I have not thought of this before. That is what insightful writing does, I guess. It taps into what is buried, but there all the same. It sounds simple, yet it's profound. It's a re-cognition.

Interestingly, I had a similar introduction to astrology as Rikki, when I too had been given an incorrect time of birth. But, unlike Rikki, my time gave me the same Tropical and Sidereal Ascendant. I wonder if this initial change of signs is what allowed Rikki to begin to incorporate these ideas from the start, having two Ascendants in mind all the while? These interpretations have not come overnight, that's for sure. There is much wisdom in her knowledge. The essence of the Precession of the Equinoxes, and the Ages, is so clearly explained that I'm wondering why we complicate it so much! Rikki's clever turn of phrase may express her Sidereal Gemini Ascendant, but her Cancerian Tropical Ascendant comes through her careful, considered approach, along with a poetic sensitivity.

Reading this book I felt as if I have unlocked an intricate puzzle, turning it over, where all of a sudden, a new vantage point is revealed. The answer reveals what was always there, within. This is clearly explained by Rikki by using each planet's placement in both their 'old' and 'new' positions, referring to Tropical and Sidereal positions.

It's as if I have opened a new level of a game I've been playing for so long, not knowing there was another level. And there it is! So many more possibilities open up. It's an absolute wonder and joy to read Rikki's explanations. Her uncanny interpretations of planetary positions, both Tropical and Sidereal, are clear and succinct. Yet the most insightful part is how they interact, as they overlap. Rikki's insights here are gold.

It would be understandable to simply skip to the positions of the planets in your own birth chart – I certainly did - but astrologers would benefit by taking time with each 'old' and 'new' interpretation. I will certainly incorporate the ideas here in my own astrological work. Rikki's knowledge, coupled with a poetic, fun, almost prose-like writing style, is also a joy to explore. I found myself smiling in recognition often. All the misalignment issues of the previous level of this 'game' now make sense. Everything falls into place.

I used to think of 'both zodiacs' as two different perspectives of the same thing. But now, thanks largely to Rikki's writing, I see that both zodiacs add something to the other. It's not only a different perspective, a fully fleshed out image is formed. My perspective has gone from a 2D image on the screen of my mind, to a 3D interactive game. I have found much joy and playfulness here. My mind, along with the zodiac, has certainly been opened by reading this book. Although it has taken me years to open to another perspective, the recognition itself is instant. All planetary positions are re-contextualized, re-imagined, seen clearly, fully, for the first time.

My wish for you, dear reader, is that you find as much wonder and awe as I, when exploring these 'old' and 'new' ideas as you flesh them out for yourself. Looking to the previous signs, if you are used to looking at your Tropical signs, your astrology, and your being, will be enriched. Looking to the subsequent signs, if you only look at your Sidereal signs, will offer the same riches. It's a win-win.

Gary O'Toole January 2022, Galway, Ireland

SIDEREAL AND TROPICAL ZODIACS WITH THEIR OVERLAP

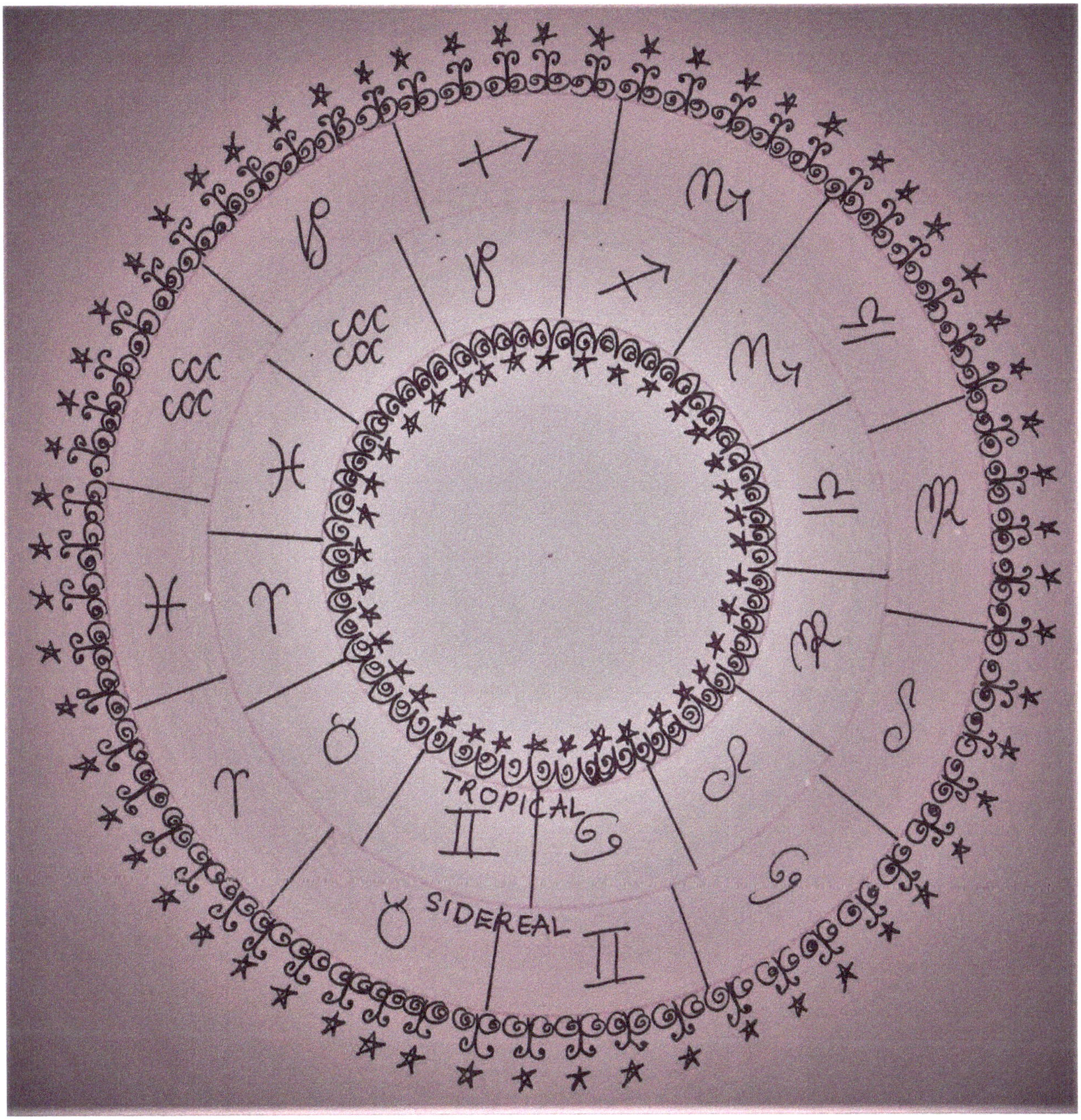

THE 24 DISTINCTIONS

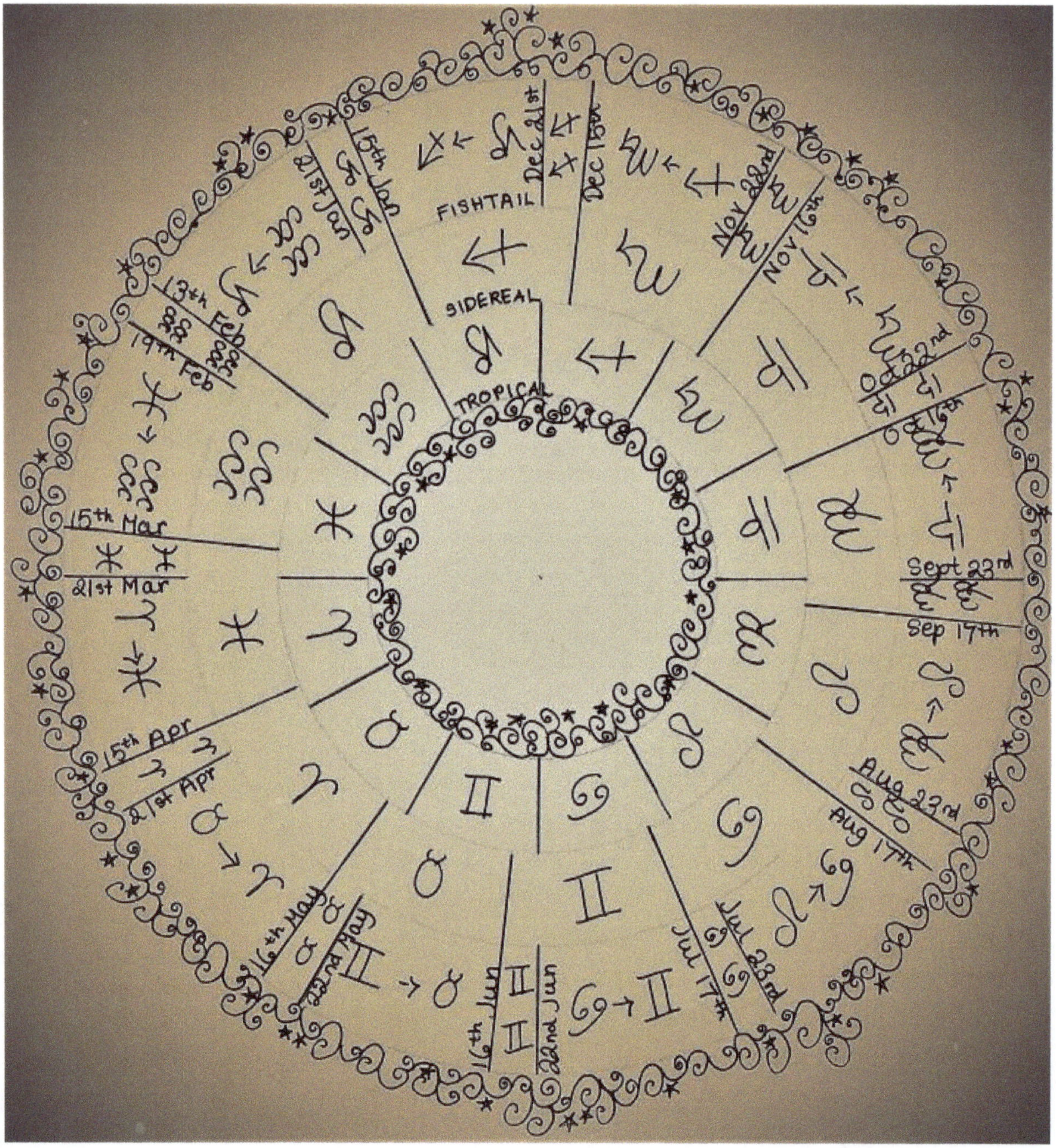

TEMPLATE FOR THE 24 DISTINCTIONS FOR ANY HOROSCOPE

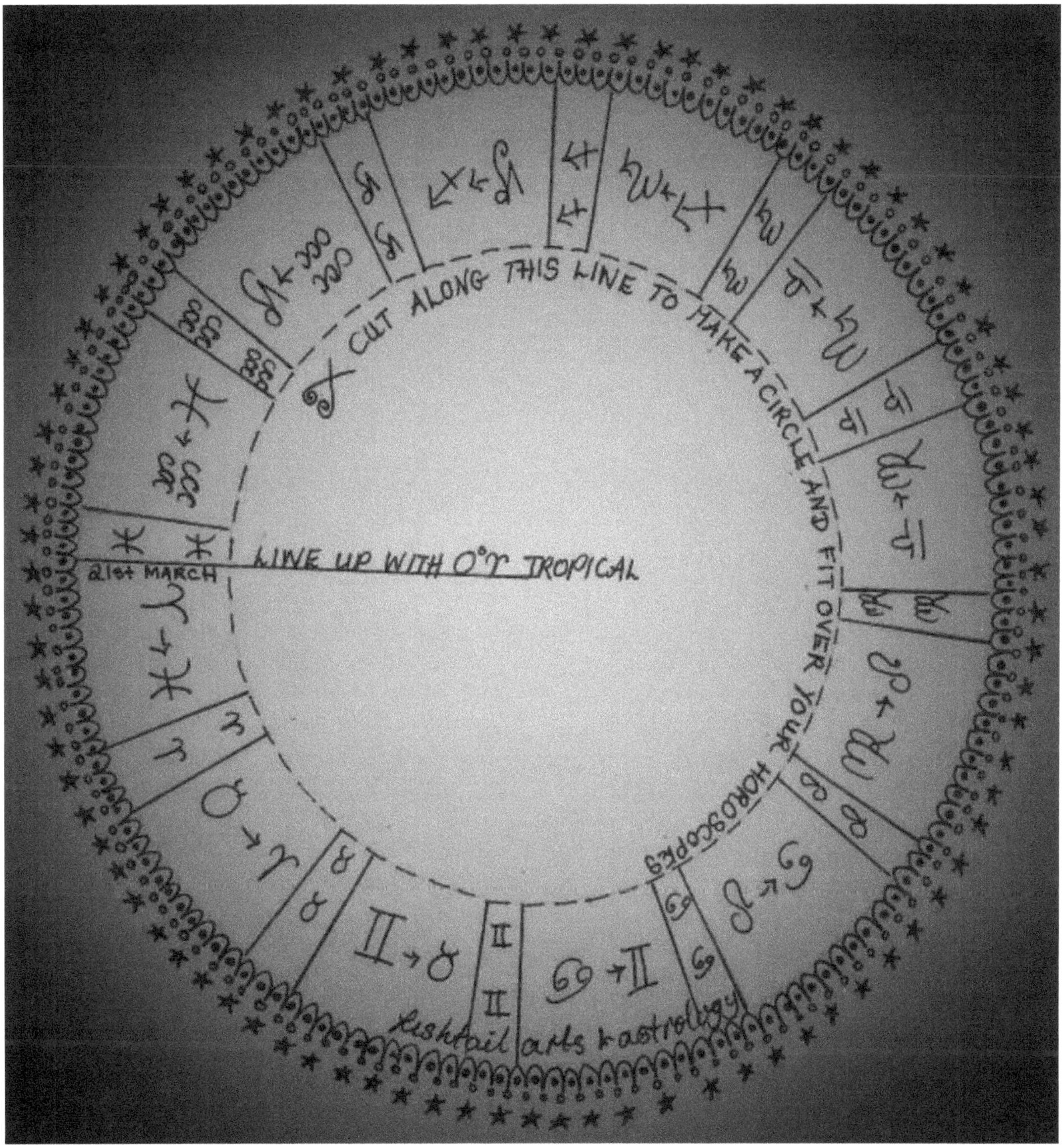

INTRODUCTION

Decades ago I walked down Caledonian Road with my baby girl in a pushchair. The Sun made sharp shadows and the heat in London was fierce that day. I was exhausted crossing town; getting on and off buses, carrying my baby, folding the pushchair up, putting her back in the pushchair, waiting for the next bus...but I felt thrilled. The Sun was shining out of me. I passed some drunken men, three of them, from young to old. The old guy called out to me, wanted to see my baby. I was so happy that day as I was going to the Urania Trust library. I was on a mission to understand the Sidereal zodiac, take notes and read Cyril Fagan's' 'Primer of Sidereal Astrology'. I had read about this book in the footnotes of another book, when studying why the constellations I could see in the sky weren't where I thought they should be. So I stepped over to him smiling; I was in my element, on an expedition to uncover what seemed like secrets of astrology. The inebriated men were 'happily sad' and lazy on a bench. I remember thinking, 'if only they had astrology...' The facet of me that is aware of all time was with me; so great was the day I began my explorations into the structure of astrology. But I hadn't been prepared for how Cyril Fagan's book would rock my view of astrology because by the end of that day I would have to choose between the Sidereal and the Tropical zodiac. It was like losing my virginity; I could never go back.

Perhaps it is just a coincidence but when I first got into astrology my mum gave me the wrong birth time, by an hour. The hospital gave me the exact time. So at first I thought I was a Gemini Ascendant. This was great by me; it explained my friendliness, talkativeness, interest in others and outgoing personality. I was rather proud to be a Gemini Ascendant. But with the correction I discovered I was a Cancerian Ascendant. I was disappointed. They were the wimps of the zodiac. However, within two days I had to admit, yup, I see my Cancerian

Ascendant. It explained my sense of vulnerability, my moodiness, I could see Cancerian Ascendant in action when I felt the urge to walk to the side when entering a room full of people and actually, it freed me. I felt a relief, like I was given more space to be me. So when faced with the choice of Sidereal or Tropical I chose Tropical; because Sidereal would give me a Gemini Ascendant and I had already felt the connection with the Tropical Cancerian Ascendant.

But I had to try and make sense of the fact that I had believed I was indeed Gemini Ascendant at the beginning; thus begun this book.

DOES THE OTHER ZODIAC MATTER?

I think of astrology as a hidden world; an occult world. You have to get into it to understand it. And the lack of understanding of astrology is one of the problems with the sceptics and scientists who hate astrology; they won't get into it so they bag it all up together. Yet astrology is made up of different cycles and the different cycles stem from different mechanisms. The main mechanisms are constellations and Planets. The constellations and the Planets have different 'properties'. They are like two separate parts of the hidden world of astrology. Just as sky and ground are two different parts of our Earth world, constellations and Planets are different parts of the astrology-world. You wouldn't expect to be able to jump in the sky and you wouldn't expect to float on the ground. Planets and constellations have different properties in our psyche; though they support each other so it looks like Planets and constellations work as one.

Astrologers have kept Planets and constellations yoked together too – and of course we use them together. But we need to separate the constellations from the Planets to see how the different parts work. In seeing how the different parts work we get to see the phenomenon of the message from the constellations and also, an inroad into proving astrology[1]. When you separate the constellations and the Planets you see that the constellations give us a 'psychological' model from which to discover the parts of ourselves that are in alignment with the universe; while the Planets prod us into 'action'. The Planets make us effective; like we are affected to be given the power of a catalyst.

In this book we are going to look at the constellations and their interpretations in both zodiacs. Whether we use Sidereal or Tropical zodiacs the constellations of the natal horoscope enable us to hone our investigation by using a 'filter' to find the House or Planet. The filter or interpretation of the constellation is like a lodestone to find a characteristic or behaviour that is buried in our soul. We use interpretation to access unconscious behaviour. We use interpretation to *find* the behaviours. Without interpretations we have only got knowledge that such and such behaviours and characteristics exist but we need to catch them in action as it were – hear the self-talk not presume the self-talk; astrology gives a wonderful model for us to *find* these conceptual parts of ourselves.

The constellations of the natal horoscope are an imaginative representation of a wheel going around the Earth. Precession of the Equinoxes shows the one wheel with different starting points. (Details of how the Precession of the Equinoxes creates 2 zodiacs will be found in the appendix.) We now have 2 separate dates to pin $0°♈$. This gives us the Sidereal and the Tropical zodiac. Essentially, yes; they both work. We are expressions of

---

[1] Astrologers have tried to prove astrology countless times through using behaviour and characteristics defined by the constellations yet repeatedly the results have been sketchy. However, the Planets, through transits and through synastry with another person's horoscope are tangible events that can be monitored and recorded. But transits are individual 'events', which is why I have created Cosmic Journal for individuals to calculate when a transit will occur; including written guidance concerning where to look and what to look for. Therefore astrology's assertion that the Planets affect us can be verified by individuals who are not necessarily astrologers.

both of the zodiacs – at the very least. In fact we are everything. But we use the zodiac to 'find' a part of ourselves that does not need to be noticed. We are looking for a state of mind, a train of thoughts, a way of thinking. And that is the point of the constellations in astrology. Unlike the Planets which move and inspire us, prod and instigate events, the constellations are like the chords in the background of the melody.

And ironically, it is the presence of the Sidereal zodiac that has revealed the premise as to why both zodiacs work. Precession of the Equinoxes, is not just the sceptics' main weapon, it is the very astronomical reality which reveals the universe has a grand design.

GRAND DESIGN

The presence of the Sidereal zodiac gives us a 2nd evolving date to begin 0°♈. These dates are 21st March for the Tropical and 15th April for the Sidereal, though as you know each year is slightly different in relation to the solar year which marks the days of our calendar, so you have to check the ephemeris each year.

The grand design is revealed through the Ages that have passed through time as well as from the actual betterment of individuals. Astrology is like a handbook for connecting with a grand design. The Ages show humanity improving through time and astrology measures that improvement in astrological principles. Though exactly what the grand design is would be foolish of me to presume but I can share some of the pointers I feel are obvious.

The reason there appears to be a grand design is because humanity improves and individuals improve through time. Lots of individuals make a tipping point for humanity. The answer as to why there is a grand design is deduced from the apparent presence of one. When everyone (or a tipping point of people) is individually 'connected' with the universe, they are aligned with their Will and are doing what they believe is nurtured by the Planets then they are improving themselves and humanity in accordance with the premise of the Age. You cannot deny that we as a species are improving in many ways. When there is the tipping point of people acting in this subtly new way then all that is happening on Earth is in alignment with the universe. The events on Earth are caused by humans because of our level of awareness.

When there is a tipping point of awareness – namely of being connected, individually with the universe, and of recognizing existence exists like a dream – I propose it leads to new thought and new awareness. The edge of our awareness now seems to be along the lines of tangibly being connected to the mechanics of universe (astrology) and the recognition that existence is not solid and only exists in the moment like a dream (Buddhism and Taoism). When these edges of our awareness of existence reach a tipping point – of the majority of people understanding - then I believe new awareness's will become possible. New awareness's such as 'why existence exists' and 'what gives life' will be comprehendible. At present these questions seem unfathomable. This, in my view, gives reason for a grand design to exist.

Since there is a great fear that we are connected and somehow destined with the inhumane movements of the universe many people refuse to uncover this reality of their connection. I understand that. Astrology and fate go hand in hand; but very few people get astrology, and very few people really understand fate. Let's just say that fate is not the ogre that sucks our Will and makes us victims. Instead fate is the force that makes us fearless, amazing, committed and the best we can be. And so astrology is one of the tools for us each to become our best until there is a tipping point of a perception (when everyone will agree on an idea that expresses the way the world is made up) which takes us, as a race, forward again.

The Ages show us a progression of humanity. We cannot deny that from 10,000 BC to now there has been betterment and improvement of the individual within the whole. Before then we don't have much data and even the stuff I will say to interpret the Ages from 12000 years ago is really only made up to enhance the premise that humanity improves over time. We do not need astrology to see this fact but for astrological purposes I shall interpret the betterment of humanity through the model of the astrological Ages.

WISDOM OF THE AGES

It is like each of the Ages has a 'Bible of Wisdom' for humanity. This wisdom is 'imparted' through the collective unconscious – the 12th House - and the 12th House gives the name of the Age. So where we see 0°♈ on the celestial equator on 21st March we see too that Pisces is fully in residence in the 12th House. So we called this Age (the one we are in still) the Age of Pisces.

As an aside – though I must mention it here as it is highly relevant; some people have said we are in the Age of Aquarius. Now where did that come from! Astronomically and Sidereally we still have 6 – 8 more degrees of Pisces above the celestial equator on the 21st March. The Sidereal zodiac has not totally over-thrown the Tropical. And yet there has been kerfuffle that we are in the Age of Aquarius.

This erroneous misfortune of Age of Aquarius related titles was created from 4th and 5th February 1962 when all the visible Planets were in Aquarius – in the Tropical zodiac. In the Sidereal zodiac they were all in Capricorn because none of the Planets were beyond 24° Aquarius. And it was apparently written 'somewhere' that the Kali Yuga would end when all the Planets were in Capricorn. Yuga means 'an age'. But the Yuga's are a different system of Ages. They are not the Ages created by Precession of the Equinoxes.

So what is important about 24° you say. Well, the Sidereal zodiac has not completely misplaced the Tropical zodiac. There is still the 6 – 8 degrees above the celestial equator. That is 6° for the Sidereal zodiac or 8° according to the sky maps and the boundaries accorded to Pisces by astronomers. This means we still have 400 odd years left of the Age of Pisces, which is a great thing, because the Age of Pisces has improved humanity immensely.

Let us look at the Ages and how they have improved humanity. We shall begin 12000 years ago, in the Age of Leo. Of course there were many Ages before this time but this will give us a good idea of the effect of the Ages and the constellations. Also, I am just giving an approximate 2000 years for each Age as it is the overall idea of the teachings of a constellation I want to convey.

10000BC In the Age of Leo the Earth got hotter! The Sun appeared stronger after the interruption to the natural warming, caused possibly by a comet crash or a volcanic eruption blocking Sun's rays. 12000 years ago the Earth got hotter as it came out of the ice age.

8000BC 10000 years ago is the Age of Cancer when ice melted and waters rose, people stopped migrating because seas and rivers separated land. They stayed at home!

6000BC 8000 years ago communities, cultures and countries began to form; networking for trade and communications began to enable people to mix. This was the Age of Gemini.

4000BC In the Age of Taurus 6000 years ago jewellery began to be made from gold. Value systems of material wealth and comfort began to be formed.

2000BC 4000 years ago in the Age of Aries anyone could be the leader if they were strong enough and had a big enough army. Leaders started to take over other leaders.

285AD[2] and the Age of Pisces; thankfully we are still in the Age of Pisces. People became compassionate. The concept of love became stronger. Humanity has grown from the middle ages where people like Count Vladimir Dracula and his guests thought it was an acceptable thing to impale people while they banqueted. In other areas of the globe people were hung, drawn, quartered, 'just' hung, heads chopped off, hands cut off – disgusting inhumane practices that now I think we as a human race can all agree is not something we should ever go back to. Compassion of Pisces has swept the globe. And with another 432 years left of the Age of Pisces I am sure there is more compassion to squeeze from humanity.

Taking the concept of the 12th House teaching humanity one step further we can see that each constellation has a kind of bible. Each constellation has a way of thinking that is PART OF A GRAND DESIGN OF OUR MINDS.

The Bible of Aries could be something like; if you want to succeed do everything you can. Be assertive. Be daring. Take action. Whereas the Bible of Taurus will be; secure your home, save money, collect valuables; create value! Look at the Bible of Gemini: to find happiness you must network and have lots of friends. Be interested in others.

The Bible of Cancer: charity begins at home. The love of the mother is divine. Happiness comes from caring for others.

The Bible of Leo; be creative. Free your inner child. Enjoy the glory, you deserve it.

The Bible of Virgo: Early to bed, early to rise, makes a person healthy, wealthy and wise. Cleanliness is next to godliness.

The Bible of Libra: where there is discord, let me bring peace; where there is hatred let me bring love. I choose how to respond

---

[2] 18th May 285 is when Lahiri Ayanamsa is calculated from. This date is said to be the beginning of the Age of Pisces. There are different Ayanamsas; calculated from different beginning times.

to the conflicts around me so I do not perpetuate a world of conflicts.

The Bible of Scorpio: find your passion! Be fierce and protect the truth that is uncovered when you look beneath the surface.

The Bible of Sagittarius: if you can imagine it you can create it. Dream big and enthusiastically go for what you believe in.

The Bible of Capricorn: keep going. If you don't stop you will get there in the end. Create rules and structures so you can keep going.

The Bible of Aquarius: everyone deserves what everyone else has. Human rights and global awareness bring happiness for all.

The Bible of Pisces; compassion for all beings and connecting to the universe brings peace on Earth. There is no need to ever fight.

All of the 'Bibles' are like parts of ourselves we need to develop to be the best human we can. Astrology shows us THESE characteristics are the ones we need.

The characteristics as defined by the constellations are the very characteristics needed for an individual to develop and to become a fully rounded actualized human being. It is the characteristic within the constellation that is the value. And since we all have everything within our own charts we can use the chart to develop these parts of ourselves.

However the crux of this book was that the zodiacs both work. You are as much your Sidereal zodiac sign as you are your Tropical zodiac sign because the Sidereal zodiac is rooted in the Tropical zodiac.

Just as we have seen that the Ages flowed into betterment for humanity we can see that the constellations flow into each other. The Sidereal zodiac is born out of the Tropical zodiac like the Tropical zodiac was born out of the zodiac from the previous Age. It is a process. And the process is the very reason both zodiacs work.

When the characteristic of the Tropical constellation is taken to its nth degree it transmutes into the characteristics of its Sidereal counterpart.

TRANSMUTATION OF THE NTH DEGREE

Everything changes in time. There is not one thing which can continue being the same; and since energy cannot be created or destroyed, when the time of its perfection has been reached – whatever it is – it changes and transmutes into another form. We see it in the natural physical world and it is there in behaviours too. Behaviours change over time.

Imagine your typical Tropical Aries person; impatient and assertive. They initiate action after action to fulfil their goal, or if they are working for someone else they do all that needs to be done, with gusto. If someone was to always push on, always be assertive they would exhaust themselves and others would resent them too. So how can that very same person be Piscean; typically passive and compassionate? Well, that assertive person exhausts all possibilities. They try everything. Then they say, 'I have done everything I can; now I must see what happens.' Isn't that the Piscean attitude in a nutshell? And the compassion comes from the 'I can, I will, I am' attitude taken to its nth degree again. When you reach out constantly for what you want you realize others are not doing the same as you or they want something different or they want what you want. The awareness of others brings the natural compassion for other humans. It is that simple.

All of the following interpretations of the Sidereal and the Tropical are based on the premise of the 'bible' of that constellation taken to the nth degree. No characteristic can continue being more and more of what it is before it has to end and change; flow into another behaviour. This is true of everything in the world as well as behaviours. In simpler terms, anger reaches a peak then subsides. But not every characteristic or behavioural trait is subject to transmuting to the preceeding sign; only the 'protected' traits; the ones that are part of the 'bible' of that sign.

Righteousness is an example of a 'non-protected' trait. Righteousness doesn't belong with any sign. It is an aberration of ego and intelligence. When righteousness is acted out again and again, when it is unrelenting, righteousness becomes proselytizing; and if proselytizing continues it becomes more and more like nagging and then an obsession and then delusion. Whereas the lovely trait of enthusiasm as often seen in Sagittarius, can continue when taken to its nth degree; when enthusiasm continues it becomes self-belief, faith and then the silent knowing of Scorpio.

Throughout this book you will discover the 'protected' traits of the constellations and you will see how they transmute as they turn into their Sidereal counterpart. I have given examples for each constellation accommodating each of the Planets. The varied examples will help you contemplate the nth degree further, to make them your own.

The 6° that have not yet been precessed are naturally more potent in the behavioural traits of that one sign; they are Sidereally and Tropically the same sign and will, second by second, year by year, transmute to the Sidereal by 1° every 72 years.

It is also important to point out that the traits that are transmutable are the very traits that are needed for the betterment of an individual and for humanity. We need them all. That is why it is good to work with the whole of the zodiac in your horoscope; finding all the characteristics.

It would take another book to pinpoint the very traits that lead to the betterment of the individual and therefore the betterment of humanity; but honestly, I feel we all know what they are. Even so, one day somebody will clarify them. For now though we can think that the specific protected traits are hidden, or mixed within the common ways of the constellations. For this book a few of the traits of each constellation will be taken to their nth degree so you can imagine more of how some behaviours transmutes to another; because it is our work as astrologers, mystics, cosmic travellers – people on this planet!- to become the person we want to become. By our own judgement of ourselves, we come to know ourselves; not by the experiences we have had but the reactions to the experiences we came across.

You are everything. And because you are everything you need a guide to find specific parts. Astrology is your guide. Your natal horoscope shows you where to look in your life to see any specific or sought after trait in action. You might have a particular trait in any area of your life but astrology tells us you are *bound* to find it in so and so constellation and House.

UNITING THE ZODIACS

As you can see from the diagram of Sidereal and Tropical zodiacs, the Sidereal zodiac is 24° 'behind' the Tropical. That means there are still 6° which are 'pure'. So there are 12 plus 12 different areas which I have called 'Distinctions.' There are 24 Distinctions. There are 6° of each constellation which are of the same constellation in both the Tropical and Sidereal zodiacs and there are 12 areas of the zodiac which are 24° each; these 24° are the part of each constellation in the Tropical zodiac which has been precessed by the Sidereal zodiac.

We now have 24 areas of the zodiac. 12 are 24° long and 12 are 6° long. The 24° and the 6° areas alternate. I have called them Distinctions.

For those of you who noticed the similarity between the 24 separate areas and the 24° for the precession I will add that the length of the area of the zodiac that is being precessed by the Sidereal – which is currently 24° - is changing by 1° every 72 years. It will be another 50 years or so until the precessed part is 25° long. And then 26°, 27° etcetera; until eventually each whole sign of the Tropical zodiac has been precessed. And then the process starts again; the first sign's characteristics are taken to the nth degree again...or maybe the synchronicity of '24' is because now is the time to look at astrology in a way that keeps astrology alive for all the Ages ahead...

24 DISTINCTIONS AND HOW TO USE THEM

This book will take you through each of the Distinctions. Each Distinction has a 'new' Sidereal sign and an 'old' Tropical sign; like a first and a middle name of the same person. In this system I have used the terminology of 'old' and 'new' because old has wisdom in it and new has energy.

By using the 24 Distinctions in this way you can see where you are resonating more with your Sidereal or Tropical characteristics. **However, by far the more immediate way of using this system is in connecting with your sense of destiny.** Find 6°♓ Tropical in your horoscope. This is the degree that is currently on the vernal equinox on 21st March. This, in the system of the 24 Distinctions is the area known as Old Pisces/New Pisces and represents our Spirit of the Age. Where does the Spirit of the Age fall in your horoscope? Can you align the goals of this house to the Spirit of the Age? 6°♓ is becoming 5°♓ as we speak. This is our time which at every Vernal equinox our soul feels the reminder. Just like at the Autumn Equinox 6°♍ is our guide in the horoscope. At the summer solstice, 6°♊ is our re-alignment guide to the Spirit of the Age and at the winter solstice it is 6°♐ that we can look to in our horoscope to find the Spirit of our Age. At these times of the year, where the corners of the world fall in your natal horoscope, what are your concerns and your goals? I propose that these degrees, which are shrinking to 5° as the precession takes over, are the edges of growth; *the frontiers of humanity.*

Another way to use these Distinctions is to find their House and planetary guests in your own horoscope and relate the Bible of the Grand Design in your own way to your own life. This way you have everything you need, at your disposal, to align with all you choose to be.

In the following detailed descriptions of the 24 Distinctions I have called Venus 'she' and Mars 'he'. I like to think of it as 'finding the man in me' and 'finding the woman in me'. So I use Mars and Venus as archetypes to lead, guide and hone these socially modified sexual energies, allowing me to interpret them more fluidly and in context for my situation.

24 DISTINCTIONS

ESSENCE OF THE 24 DISTINCTIONS

Pisces Pisces ~ deepening compassion
Pisces Aquarius ~ sharing compassion
Aquarius Aquarius ~ global unity of individuals
Aquarius Capricorn ~ reforming society
Capricorn Capricorn ~ maintaining worthy traditions
Capricorn Sagittarius ~ strengthening different cultures
Sagittarius Sagittarius ~ finding new ways
Sagittarius Scorpio ~ protecting truths
Scorpio Scorpio ~ understanding motivations
Scorpio Libra ~ real rather than nice
Libra Libra ~ peaceful civility
Libra Virgo ~ peace and health
Virgo Virgo ~ healthful practices
Virgo Leo ~ vitality and creativity
Leo Leo ~ encouraging strength
Leo Cancer ~ protecting the feminine
Cancer Cancer ~ safe retreats
Cancer Gemini ~ networking the sweetness
Gemini Gemini ~ passing on the message
Gemini Taurus ~ win/win values
Taurus Taurus ~ symbolic comforts
Taurus Aries ~ achieving worthy goals
Aries Aries ~ choosing what is wanted
Aries Pisces ~ wanting others to have choice

OLD ARIES/NEW PISCES

Old Fire – New Water

Condensed spirit glistens - silence; first rays of light.
Daring to act on inspirations.

A specific trait of Aries is daring action. They are the people who 'just do it'. They are assertive; they make things happen. Assertiveness and daring, bravery and courage, this is the behaviour needed for you to stand up for truth. Yet action following action following action cannot continue; yin yang, light follows dark, waves rise and fall; there must be rest in between. This is the rest of Pisces; the retreat of passivity, going with the flow, 'I have done all I can now I shall wait and see.' The Pisces traits of passivity and waiting and non-action are only relevant to our betterment when the right action *has* been taken. There is an important time to rest, sit back, wait and let things be; after daring and assertive action has cut the ice.

The people born with their Ascendant here weigh successes and challenges against a gnawing feeling that there is more to life than success; though what is more valuable than a result is hard for them to define. At least aiming to win alleviates that confusing strange yearning, while the energy of Pisces swishes everything material into the path of the incoming tide. They know their goal is not materialistic. They have to keep re-evaluating their motives. Most of the people born as Aries in the Tropical Zodiac were born under Sidereal Pisces. Their confident, wilful and daring Ascendants are easy to spot; their ability to go into a new situation without being crippled by doubts is innate confidence carried over from the past. Aries are known as energetic people who face life fearlessly. They are in tune with their golden spirited energy and trust something in themselves which doesn't depend on the outside. Pisces influence is subtle and obvious when you look. There is a kind of heroic way that they do everything they can and then they sit back and wait. They say, 'whatever will be, will be.'

Old Aries/New Pisces Suns are sensitive to others and put a lot of energy into helping those they love. They do not give themselves enough credit for being somebody who gets things done because they are not as go-getting as they feel they *should* be. No-one could begrudge them any of their dreams as they are never cruel in going for what they want; often apologetic should they have to say 'no' or 'go' to someone, that's why they are good sports people too. Also, they are very team spirited – because a great team needs great individuals and they see the best in people and in themselves. The stars of New Pisces have inspired compassion whilst they are running in pursuit of their goals. The wisdom from the stars of Pisces coupled with the old Arian knowledge gives greater confidence to live their dreams, visions and wishes. Old Aries/New Pisces Suns have dreams that are close to consciousness and they grow up believing they must live their dreams. They use the power and energy invested in them to go for their dreams; they follow something deeper, something sent from the depths of their being, perhaps even from their past; a seed that has taken a lifetime to germinate. Their shameless belief in themselves is part of the ideal solar nature and why the Sun is said to be exalted in Aries.

New Pisces that is also Aries - Sun and Moon - has a capacity for martyrdom yet because of Aries they are unlikely to be anyone's rug. They have much to give and they know it; often finding it easier to take care of others more than themselves. Like a child they can forget to count their own face. Though they are Old Aries so if anyone forgets them, then they notice! Pisces' influence is the blurring of the boundaries between me and you. Old Aries rests in the just being of Pisces, recouping for a battle worth fighting for.

The Moons, at this Distinction of the zodiac, are very loving but they have that coldness of perhaps not feeling warm and loved enough; deep down they feel raw. Instead they act in ways like only fun would make them happy. They are very clear about happy and sad and what they want but this vulnerable Moon can go too fast in trying to get what they need. Often what you get is an angry Moon who has sore feet because they got too close, gave too much and someone trod all over them. These Moons can give too much then feel bereft so they buckle up and step out to have a good time. They make their own good times and this is their knowledge, how to muscle up, move on and make the most of life. They are often the first to volunteer. They have high energy levels and feel they can help ten times better than anyone else; then they get overloaded, crash and set everything alight around them. The old red Moon mixed with the new Rainbow Moon learns to enjoy its own bounty without guilt or shame; it doesn't have to share everything. They honour the kindness and compassion they have already, willingly offered.

Sometimes Mercury in Old Aries has enough opinions to fill a room, and if you want to add something you better be quick or right or ready to stand up for your ideas with the energy most people would save for dangerous situations; otherwise you will be made to see the loopholes, flaws and woolly thinking of your argument. Old Aries' Mercury has a lot of ideas and opinions which seem to be more important than the person. Ideas are the fuel for action. Ideas are worth fighting for. Yet when Pisces has its influence, the opinionated and idealistic judgements over every little thing is balanced with recognizing their opposition has feelings too; well, at least they recognize old people, children and animals need a bit more care. They are open to your viewpoint though – if it is watertight.

Venus in Old Aries was not particularly fussed about how she looks, preferring excitement and new challenges but it didn't take long to realise when she looked good people responded in a way that noticed her more. And Venus in Old Aries wants to be noticed. New Pisces has brought with it a far more relaxed feeling – the very essence of just feeling lovely all by itself, whatever she wears or whatever the situation. Pisces gives Venus the grace to be inactively magnetic and dissolves the drive to *do* something attractive. Venus in Old Aries had rushed away from her childhood, rushed to be grown and sexually powerful but New Pisces can re-thread that past, and lead Old Aries back down the winding path to pick up all the loose ends of a life spun in fast forward, to live more gently and deeply as they get older. This placement is one of rejuvenation when one is older. It can be likened to drinking Water from the fountain of youth, the spirit of which never left them; then one day they look back and see how much more each moment had to offer and going back, drinking from their past, they release deep emotions and relaxing more, years drop from the lines in their face.

Mars in Old Aries/New Pisces was one of the combinations that alerted me to the discovery of the unity of Tropical and Sidereal Astrology. I noticed just how easily distracted this placement could be. It was never as dynamic, or as challenging as I had expected. Of course, these people were easily flagged or riled, and distraction is a typical feature of Mars in Aries. Yet I could not help but notice how many times they seemed to shrug their shoulders and walk away. On probing further I found not everything was worth the fight. Naturally they fought for some things, like principles and children and things weaker than themselves were a favourite, as was fighting against things – situations and organisations bigger than themselves. There is a distinct drive towards battles and fights and challenges for the benefit of others. But many stepped back rather than risk friendships (in their opinion) when they could have had a good natured challenge. Their Will and determination goes into a whirlpool of caring for others. Old Aries/New Pisces Mars has to ensure its Will actually achieves something positive so the energy doesn't fall back down the hole again.

Jupiter in Aries was always considered a bit of a waste of energy. With dynamo Aries the exaltations were exaggerated and the finer qualities of Jupiter's higher mind got scattered. This was the view of Tropical Aries – the Old Aries we know so well, so it must be the effect with Jupiter in Sidereal Pisces as well as in Tropical Aries. The Piscean stars are in harmony with the energies of Jupiter, we know that from the original astrologers, yet over the years the mystical vibration of Jupiter in Pisces has been scorned by the 'doers' in society. Jupiter in Pisces is the essence of many religions; it is the precept of compassion. The development of compassion with wisdom comes precisely from meditation, and focussing deeply on one thing for a period of time. The benefit from Jupiter in Pisces needs an energetic and determined mind. The union of compassion with wisdom cannot be attained by the low-lit light of consciousness; it needs to be full on. Jupiter in Old Aries/New Pisces is up for the challenge of focusing on not focusing. They tread the path to enlightenment like a Sherpa across the Himalayas.

Saturn in Old Aries or New Pisces put on a front. They pretend to bc brave even if they are not and in the words of Pooh to Piglet "for a very small animal to only blinch inside is a brave thing". The positive side of New Pisces housing Saturn is silent bravery and self-responsibility to do the things they must. Saturn in Old Aries/New Pisces is most fearful in situations in which they should *relax*, act naturally and go with the flow. They are far more suited to daring themselves to do something, whether an exam, unplanned meeting with their boss, or climbing Mount Everest; in these situations their daring is obvious. But having to act naturally in the company of peers is its limit. In fact, letting go and going with the flow in any situation is hard for this placement. So the assertive Aries' bravado leaps to the fore and they only blinch inside until social ease becomes their strength.

OLD ARIES/NEW ARIES

Old Fire - New Fire

A fresh flame drops, heats the Air, scorches the Earth, recoils from the sea. Too late; make a wish.

These natives typify Aries and all we have come to know of Aries. They say things like "shy bairns get nought" while others say of them, "they aren't backward in coming forward!" Though there are many people to whom such forthright behaviour could refer to, there are not so many whom are daring, explorative and challenging without anger. Anger is the mark of those who feel resentment at their inability to express themselves. Aries/Aries Ascendants just express themselves; the world is exciting, it is quite dangerous in places but they are up for the challenge. A strange description of this Ascendant is that they are very loving. They love life; they love people, though they aren't particularly gentle. They love life with a passion that is the core of their spirit to go out every day to give life a go and make their best effort. These people are one of the least unlikely to get depressed as their zest for challenges comes from a very deep level. The danger is in not having a plan or project to put everything into. And as long as they sometimes step down from their charging horse and walk carefully when the ledge is thin and slippery, these Ascendants remain buoyant and eager.

The powerful effect of this Sun is obvious to see. People born at this time are most definitely wilful, brave and daring. I would even say that the few days leading up to this starry influence has an effect of increasing assertiveness. This is a learned confidence of winning - as the native knocks up one challenge after another. They are motivated by stories of heroism, bravery and exploration and from a young age they grow in confidence; understanding themselves as braver and more determined to win than most; not that they are particularly boastful, it is just something they know and accept about themselves. They feel it is their mission to be the one that champions their friends and their siblings and all they care about; if not, the world will fall apart and they would blame themselves for not having done enough about it. If anything, they expect too much from themselves. Naturally, they are attracted to people who in other ways have stood up for what they believed in. As a friend, these people are at your side like a body guard defending or attacking – whatever needs to be done - to ensure their confidante is at their most motivated. That's what they can't stand, giving up. These people are hard on themselves because their inner sense of belief is so strong they just know they are somehow tougher than others and should therefore live up to their own expectations. They have sussed out which rules can be dispensed with and that's what makes them exciting people; they don't waste time going around unnecessary obstacles.

The karmic lessons of Old Aries reveal a nature that kept things spontaneous with no routine, which is an anathema to the traditional Moon. From youth to old age the Moon craves routine but here it has learned to live without and now it must learn to thrive in such inhospitable soil. This is a hard placement for the Moon to be born into but it doesn't mean it cannot thrive, it can. The Moon here must discover the essence of itself. Underneath the set patterns of bedtime and dinnertime is the wild hunting Moon. The wild hunting Moon has almost no place in our society which further throws this nature back upon itself, but still all is not lost. The hunting nature of old was to grab what it can, whereas now, in our organised society of supermarkets open 24/7 this Moon can go anywhere. It can reach and touch the bottom of the ocean, dry in the Sun then stop off and get a vegan-sausage roll before racing over plains of prairie grass. The forward driving lesson for this Moon is to listen to what it fancies. Hunt for what it will. Get what it likes. This sounds a rather hedonistic directive but only if it follows false needs. In its true form, intuition will guide this Moon to getting the food and sleep and rest that it needs whilst fitting all the other more fun things to do in its busy day. This is a low maintenance Moon that can thrive in a lifestyle that would make other Moons sick. Tempers only flare when this nature forgets to consider its real physical needs and has a boring routine. The emotional side of this Moon likes to be thrilled with a fast paced life and listening to when and what they really want; to eat/sleep/rest at *their* inner behest; that is how they can thrive in our modern world.

Mercury within these degrees bestows a mind that goes so fast that it trips over its own words as it speaks and cannot even write clearly enough it has to scribble it all down before the thoughts have gone. The intelligence of this placement is often hard to see because of the rush to get it all out. I do not think there is anything that should be done to slow this wonderfully fast and brilliant machine except utilize other aspects in their birth chart that can help channel the flow of thought and sustain more of what needs to be said first time around. Though what these people will probably always have to do is check their work and go back over it to cut out all of the asides. However, they do make great pitches, selling their ideas.

It is true I will repeat myself many times with this placement; whether Venus, Mars, Moon or Sun, the principle is the same; the high-powered drive to go for what they want colours all things the same. Here Venus is influenced to use what it has, namely her charms to get what she wants. Only she doesn't see it as manipulative, she sees it as fair game. In fact, if another was playing the same game Venus in Old Aries/New Aries would be in her element, flirting with a worthy opponent, upping the tempo and charging the Air around. Naturally she wears red and her hair is often dyed blonde as it has more effect. The cast off from Old Aries gives Planets placed here deeper confidence and daring so that even a full-bloodied Aries Venus wins her desires. She may still believe in love at first sight but foremost she believes in herself. She got dressed up, she went to the right place and she dared smile across the room and behold his eyes with her eyes for just that bit longer.

Mars in Aries/Aries is ready for action – 'right kit, right determination' could be his motto. Mars arrives with the perfect persona and a twinkle in his eye, because he's pretty sure he's going to win. Most other Mars' roll their inward eyes for the showiness of it all; but they know they are in for an exciting challenge. Old Aries has given this Mars plenty of successes and plenty more drive for new challenges. New Aries shows this Mars what the brave and daring energy of Aries can be used for; to explore things on Earth, maybe space, to go further, faster, higher, longer than most. This energy extends the successes of the human race. As a leader this energy takes responsibility for the success of his team, winning is not just posturing, winning is energy that literally crackles. It won't sit back and let old woes slip over – this is humanity at the beginning of its leap to a world with far greater medicine, knowledge, abilities and usefulness than the world we live in today. The optimism of Old Aries/New Aries is the energy needed to take the first step for massive change. This energy is easily roused; quick to take on a challenge.

Jupiter here has big dreams and with all this energy at its disposal it isn't about to let anything, not even itself, get in the way of achieving something that most people would dare not dream. The daring and competitive energy of the double Arien influence is stronger than the distractible effects of Pisces over Old Aries. Here the sense of inner confidence is unmistakeable to the native, they are not about to let opportunity slip by. These people feel they have a mission to take themselves to the edges of possibility. Whether through science or exploration or sport this placement is strengthened in confidence by the triple effect of enthusiastic energy.

Many of the karmic lessons of Old Aries covered by New Pisces apply here too but the innocence here is not so tender and gullible. This really is a placement for Saturn to overcome their fears and work within their limitations and some degree of bravery is called for. Whether it is sleeping with the door closed at night or overcoming their fear of flying by plane, the choice is theirs. It is well to remember Saturn always brings choice; to do what must be done but how you do it is up to you. So the fear needn't limit them, they can go by boat. Neither should the small dark room. Maybe they could share. Fears are only passages to go through and if there is another way round, go around. Either way, fear here has to be accepted so the native can move on. Saturn will move on whether they overcome or go around their fear; their fear of things is their motivator to success.

OLD TAURUS/NEW ARIES

Old Earth - New Fire

Light shafts beckon from the cut out triangles of the decorated clay lantern.

I am sure you know of that Taurus who decides to sell their house, at £50k more than the standard price. They know it is worth it – to them. It is undoubtedly valued higher because it is THEIR house. So they put their house on the market £50k higher than the average. And they will sit and wait. They would wait years; 5 years maybe. However long it takes, they will wait till they get their asking price. Others see them and say, 'drop the price,' 'No!' They cannot because their own sense of value is palpable, it pumps in their blood; they feel it with their breath. Then after 2 or 3 years they get frustrated. We don't call it impatience because they are Taurus; we call it frustration and notice how our Taurean friend is getting themselves all wound up. Till wham! They spend £5k on their house, they make it look £50k more and soon enough that house sells for the asking price. You see the trait of sticking to your values is an important one for the betterment of our selves but if it never changes, it becomes a fool version of itself. Old Taurus/New Aries holds out till frustration cum impatience changes its game-plan – then it becomes the Arian trait of assertiveness. Action to affect the desired outcome comes from the trait of sticking to your values.

Despite the term 'old' for the Tropical sign these Ascendants are like young bulls. They know their inner strength and determination is at hand when they want to do or not do something. With the new stars of Aries their energy is lightened, less ponderous. They are a bit frisky. A bit flirty too, like they know their sexuality shows and Aries encourages them to express that. They also like to compete and dress immaculately, for social situations are their field. They see the rules for status and wealth and are motivated to not appear needy or poor. New Aries adds the impetus to be even more self-reliant to enhance the Taurus' drive for greater security - which was already strong.

Old Taurus/New Aries are not showy people, though they do resent having to follow others. They go their own way without telling anyone. The old Taurus knowledge of sticking to get whatever they want and getting it eventually is coupled with the New Aries influence of doing more to get what they want sooner. They have learnt to practice great patience and endurance, during which time they improve their surroundings by making it as comfortable as it can be and do whatever needs to be done for their goal. When the Sun is in this position you also see the knack of stretching money, space, time, whatever they need as a means to the end that they have envisioned. I say 'end'; they have middle ends, and beginning ends, and all sorts of goals for various stages and somehow it seems they always get what they want, materially. Instinctively they are experts in manipulating matter. Now, they yearn for something that is more of a challenge. They know their mind and body is strong. They yearn to escape from the belief that everything is going to be ideal; they yearn to continue pushing on and fighting.

A lot of what was said about the Sun in Old Taurus applies for the Moon, as Taurus is so deeply knowledgeable of the material world and the Moon is deeply knowledgeable of the body in relation to its environment. Moon in Old Taurus was exalted because of the comfortable knowledge of its body and it achieved health and comfort as naturally as a fish swims and a bird flies. Now this wonderful benefit is being called upon to loosen its grip and take on a new stance when the old one was perfect. New Aries offers something more to Taurus' Moons; it offers modern life, getting into the swing of the hustle and bustle whilst still being in control of emotional stability. The world has moved on since astrology was first recorded and the slow pace associated with the Moon in Taurus is rarely even possible, though these natives probably do pare their lives down so as not to get overloaded. Yet Aries stars make these people keener to get involved with some of that exciting world we now live in. It is good for others to see how it is done, living like a Buddha in the midst of craziness, though not too crazy. These people would have departed the scene way before it becomes too crazy, they are not martyrs and instinctively they are survivalists. New Aries asks Old Taurus Moons to make a peaceful environment in an exciting one. New Aries says 'step out of your comfort zone and create some of that nourishing magic in a more challenging environment'.

With Mercury the native is challenged to think outside the box. They take on this new challenge because Old Taurus Mercury would hate to think of themselves as staid, even if they were. So they tend to read huge broadsheets from beginning to end, though they might miss out sport. They love politics, reading about it that is and reading about luxurious places to go. Business means a lot to these natives – how business changes over time, modern businesses, and modern trends. Mercury here likes to be up on what is new in the areas of life so closely connected with money, luxury and food. Mercury in Old Taurus likes to think and talk about food, diet and put new discoveries into practice too, as a proper investigation. This placement will use its own body to see if there is any truth in new ideas but not scientific and paid investigations; they wouldn't risk their body at all, just new sensible kinds of medicines, harmless yet beneficial panaceas. Business, food, health and medicines: Mercury in Old Taurus/New Aries likes to be at the forefront of knowledge in these realms.

As one of Venus' ruling domains, Old Taurus offers Venus the beauty and calm surroundings she craves. This is the innate knowledge that people born with their Venus within these degrees have; they know instinctively how to create the right atmosphere for love to flow; the atmosphere which creates passivity in the Mars nature, even in Uranian nature. Venus in Old Taurus can create an ambient situation for anything. Before, Venus in Old Taurus preferred its own home or a working environment where she may have been for most of the day every day. The influence begins in her body. Now, New Aries wants Venus to step out into new and unplanned situations more often and spread the good vibration.

This is a very happy Mars! It has found a little extra something. Its rooted strength allowed it to complete many projects but it was not recognised, except poetically, as the strong, silent type. Most with Mars here like company; to prove themselves and polish their horns with. They are hard workers, liking to go out in the world then come back to their palace; as their home life and their work life are a reflection of their supremacy. New Aries encourages more projects and Old Taurus knows how to finish them. They work well together; this native physically does more in their world than most. And they don't resent it either, their doing is their glory. Being fit and strong is their way of proving themselves. New Aries adds keenness and fast twitch muscles. This placement, with its innate knowledge of endurance and strength has been given a true zing to give it a go. They value life and champion lifestyles to protect optimum animal-like health. New Aries urges Old Taurus not to sit back in the safety and comfort of their DIY palace but to go forth and ensure their wider realm is protected.

Materialistic Jupiter in Old Taurus is inspired to manifest their vision where the most straightforward way to attain a goal is measured against the quickest. The simple plodding of Jupiter in Old Taurus became streaked with impatience. Goal orientated Jupiter is encouraged to think, then act. New Aries adds the intuition of the higher mind; the fast twitch muscles of the mind. So Old Taurus nature trusts its body response while Aries relays immediate intuitions. What use is higher knowledge if it is just baggage? Physical body knowledge has been updated with flashes of insight encouraging this native to build knowledge through experience. And under the fire of Aries even the thoughts and feelings of Taurus become physical experiences.

In the old times Saturn in Taurus was a stickler for traditions and health with safety was the be all and end all. New Aries inspires Saturn to go for the deeper things that matter instead of just sticking to the tracks of society. Old Taurus revered people with doctorates, people who have proven their endurance; 'lowly jobs don't command much respect'. But New Aries, as an advocate to individual will-power points out the benefits of work that offers freedom, spontaneity and independence; and so this native dares itself to take a different kind of job. They come down from their ivory tower and have more time to try new things.

OLD TAURUS/NEW TAURUS

Old Earth – New Earth

A mound rises from the sand; it pushes up, reaches in four directions, separating limbs; the statue unfurls.

Where the old Taurus of the Tropical zodiac was governed by Earth, new Taurus fits like a lock into the key of the old temperament. The native is comfortable, secure and tight-lipped about their contentment, which is no complacency; they work continuously to maintain their serene persona. Should a whiff of intrusion or disruption come into their orb they tighten their belt while appearing passive as they watch and wait; for years maybe – however long it takes for them to come out with no loss. New Taurus, in this Distinction, is in the place of fixity which adds a further stubbornness to the character; they know where they are going and what they are doing and by keeping their own council have no intention of explaining themselves. It is no point telling them to do things differently unless you are an expert who has succeeded in making an impressive financial advantage as these Ascendants are very aware of material status; which can include living off the land in an ideal way. Status and/or money give security. Life is very simple for these Ascendants; family, home, work, appearances, friends; they have a clear and strong value system and they just endure everything to maintain their standard.

There is a determination here that is silently ominous. These natives are doubly sure of their physical endurance and though they prefer luxury they can endure physical discomfort like a determined soldier carrying their mate across mountains. Their survival instincts are very strong. Equally strong is their determination to move heavy objects in pursuit of a better environment but they are not only about the physical realm; these natives are bestowed with an inner calmness to watch life. Calm and watching they take in all the impressions. For them it is obvious why people get stressed or unhappy while their karmic gift is to enjoy life at an elegant pace. Taurus/Taurus pares down life to include only that which is worthwhile to them. What they don't want they ignore, which is preferable to arguing; unless it is an immediate threat to their home, which is as close to their soul as a snail's shell is to the snail. It cannot be over-stated how protective Taurus Suns are of their home, despite it being just stone and cement, carpets and curtains, furniture and dishwashers. Taurus crosses the threshold of their abode and instantly feels peace and security. Without security the soul cannot relax and it is in being calm and relaxed that is the key to Taurus' influence. In turn they are a more calming influence than most because they try to be.

The home is aspected strongly with the Moon as it was for the Sun in Taurus/Taurus but it is different to the Taurus/Aries Moon who is inspired to reach out of their comfort zone. Taurus Sun reveres the home as the temple for its body, ideas, desires and projects; Taurus Moon reveres its own body for its own sake. The home is protected too but the home is recognised as dispensable whereas the body is not. The gifts of Taurus from the Tropical zodiac are the natural and unaffected desires and impulses to look after its own body. For endurance and for relaxation, the aim is to be the best equipped for life. Taurus/Taurus Moons are careful not to get ill so they eat well and keep calm. Obviously each of us should take care of our body but with Taurus/Taurus Moons astrology shows when these natives focus on this aspect they get more results from it.

Perhaps most Moons have way more to do; for instance Sagittarius needs to ensure a future course for freedom but Taurus/Taurus just needs to focus on its basic body's needs. Although Taurus/Taurus Moons seem like they have it easy, maybe to some it sounds dull; though it is the results that count. It doesn't seem exciting to be looking after what you eat and sleep and keeping calm, seems more like a chore to many but these Moons feel good and right about doing it; if they don't honour their body daily they feel lethargic and powerless.

Unlike the Mercury in Old Taurus/New Aries, business is not such a driving concern but building is. These people work with their hands, with the very foundations our modern lives are built on. The digits of their fingers are especially pronounced as their hands have explored and created materials since they were children thereby strengthening their fingers. These people like to make money, as money is the commodity that helps ensure their security and subsequent endurance but they are unlikely to go into business for themselves as they are more fearful than the earlier born natives when Aries had precessed over Taurus. Instead these natives would prefer to work as an employee of an established business. Old Taurus/New Taurus think methodically, slowly and surely yet they are not dull witted; their imagination has a practical twist and they like to think of the versatility of an abstract idea, grounding it as soon as possible with sensible conclusions. If Mercury in double Taurus was given form it would be a wooden sculpture with golden wings on his heels. He would fly only in day shunning the dark and treacherous shadows; he – the statue - would live in a stately home where he could overlook a well-kept garden. He would know the colloquial name of all the plants and encourage the gardener to grow what can be eaten. He would wake up with the Sun and go to bed at a good hour that ensured the evening was enjoyed too, as there were probably guests at dinner parties. The evening after work would be given over to pleasure rather than study and certainly no work. If these natives travel they travel in style and preferably not far in the weekdays as like to keep secure and orderly days.

Venus in Taurus/Taurus is like the Empress, surrounded by lush vegetation, family, a walled garden, fine clothes and trustworthy friends. She knows womanly wiles and channels the feminine energy through a smile which oozes sensitivity and Earthy passions. Her body is strong and supple with soft curves and fleshy love; she does not hide her body and is aware of her charms. She is comfortable in her flesh. She is kind to herself and kind to others. The double impact of Taurus on Venus takes her lustiness and charms one step further so she stars in her immediate circle. All her friends know her as the centre of their friendship; she is the epitome of loving friendship in human form. She waves her arm and the fine cloths swirls about her as she smiles and beckons her friends to relax and enjoy; for Venus in Taurus/Taurus is also focused on relaxing; relaxation being the main impetus for Tropical and Sidereal Taurus. The Venusian vibration attracts to itself what it desires. Its desirous nature is very gentle, passive and open, magnetic too. The beauty that this Venus nature feels inside surrounds her. There is a lesson for us all as we look to perfect a loving vibration, for Venus in Taurus/Taurus manifestations are easier to attain.

Mars in Taurus/Taurus: I wouldn't interfere with these guys – just let them get on with what they are doing, no amount of heaving them to get up to do your Will will work, might as well just let them do what they want. I have known these double Taurus' Mars people play sport to a high degree, as well as others who sit at home listening to midnight talk radio and potter in their garden. They do what they want. I have wondered whether outside influences have had much to do with the path they have decided upon or whether they start one way then they go that way and there is no altering that path. These natives seem to have made up their mind as young people, early 20's, after studying and spreading their wings from the family's dictates, and then they stick with it. They might continue on a family business despite the lack of money but would not willingly consider changing their path at all. The Mars energy infused with Taurus/Taurus is reliable, firm, strong, enduring; it knows itself and can trust itself so its own drive is a noticeable virtue; constant, reliable, there is no obstacle insurmountable, because time is on their side.

Jupiter here helps lighten the load. Taurus/Taurus is heavy and only the strength and magnitude of Jupiter can carry this weight like a giant helping the old man with stuffed shopping bags. Jupiter is free to come with huge ideas, exuberant plans and a breadth of vision. Jupiter is locked on to Earth with great ambitions, to concretise all that it believes in. Where Taurus of the Tropical Zodiac is covered by Sidereal Taurus the result is a more rounded Taurus influence, deeper and in tune with Gaia, universal concerns, global matters. The native here helps concretise these ideals.

Saturn in double Taurus: the desire to work is strong and enduring; they are reliable workers finding meaning in their jobs. You won't find one of these in the dole queue; if you did they'd be very depressed. Depression can hit these people if there are no chances of getting a job – even a small chance does not send them spiralling to their depths as they are so willing to endure hardship and to keep trying and applying for jobs until one comes along. These people have ensured they have valuable experience and skills; if they are a secretary they will be the most reliable, grammatically correct, honest and highly valuable secretary in the pit. If a shop assistant or a mechanic they are equally valuable to their boss; they are ambitious. Not for status – for security! Sometimes these people can be immoveable when they should be doing something. There are times a wilful stubbornness takes over and they want the world to know they are the master of their own life, and so they refuse to move. They are keeping their world the same. During such a time (of proving they are the masters of their destiny) they might be relaxing, watching TV or reading a book but they are not lazy; just plodders doing their own thing and no-one can make them do otherwise.

OLD GEMINI/NEW TAURUS

Old Air – New Earth

There are holes for doors and windows but the breath of the ancestors stays in the stone temple at the top of the hill.

Here the spirit of Gemini centres on community matters. Yet, like all the traits it cannot go on as unstoppable; meeting and talking with people, sharing ideas constantly; if it continues like this it becomes a gossip, a nag. It needs to find its way forward so it becomes a source of value. The words *sound* like treasure. You know when you hear something and it resonates; words have meaning, they have value. This shows too that the trait of sharing ideas and communicating is given to us to further ourselves and humanity. Words are also used to share and convey safety; they are not meant to be just an alarm system. New Taurus wants to build something valuable, exquisite and enjoyable and so words are used to share what is good and healthy and lovely; where you will find the gold; how you can make your life or anyone's life better. Words are meant for us to share positive values; abundance, pleasure and good fortune are meant to be shared. New Taurus shows that having a good quality of life comes when more people can have it. Trying to have a good quality of life just for yourself and maybe your inner circle is like a wonky table; it will never really feel good to sit at.

Gemini's – of the Tropical zodiac – love to talk. Of course; yes, they love to communicate in as many ways as possible. This is their innate knowledge – how to just open up a conversation. Like good Scrabble players they open the board, allow many responses but why they do it is to be sure of and to stabilise their surroundings. These Ascendants are affronted by arguments, bad vibes and too many strangers too often. Naturally they like some time with new people but only structured events and not too often. Their innate ability to open any conversation and join in is really only within the crowds and structures that they already understand. It is not this native's desire to make sure everyone feels welcomed. They want their family and friends to be welcomed. Many times I have watched Old Gemini/New Taurus silently watch new people. They show me that Tropical Gemini/New Taurus has ideas about people, preconceptions even, but preconceptions that are easily broken. They process constantly when meeting new people. They are present, in the now, pigeon holing every nuance and immediately, internally, feeding back the response; ready to take back that thought and put it in a different pigeon hole. Which again is another reason why these natives are able to communicate with an apparent diversity of people; because they have already pigeon holed ideas they had of them; it is like they already recognize some things about them.

The Sun represents our vitality and here the solar energy is renewed and strengthened when the natives are in a safe environment yet able to communicate with a variety of people. They accept everyone as different, they see our differences. Not only the looks but also the measure of our sense of humour, interests or hobbies, wit and weather, seriousness of unknown purpose or sulky nature; all of this is obvious to Old Gemini/New Taurus. And this knowledge is used to secure their corner of the world. They talk to check out what else is about. These people are excellent shopkeepers; they make people feel comfortable and special at the same time. Their use of topics such as weather, is never too boring to go over again as it is only a means to find out if their preconceptions of you were measured correctly by the things you say without directly saying. What the new stars can show Old Gemini is how to accept more of their own animal nature; they accept it in others better than they can in themselves. That is why conversations about other peoples' lives are so fascinating for them; they are human-watching. In getting to understand others they understand themselves. Ultimately they want to express their taste and opinions.

Of course, we all need people who are interested in us but for Old Gemini/New Taurus Moons it is a living hell to be in an environment where they are not acknowledged intellectually and daily. Other Moons may be comfortable just being comfortable, or cooked for or even being with someone they do not see too often but Old Gemini/New Taurus Moons need to feel noticed with valuable ideas, even if what they talk about is not quantum anti-matter or any other in-depth subject. They need the security of understanding and being understood by the people around them. Only after mental closeness has been proved over time does this Moon relax *physically*. Old Gemini Moon is sensitive to smells too and the New Taurus Moon makes a big deal out of perfumery and other evocative and alluring scents.

Of course this Mercury likes to talk but only on subjects they feel particularly safe with. Many of these people say, even as adults, they dread going to parties alone or being in a situation when they know nobody, though trines can help dealing with an overwhelming number of impressions; still these natives are unlikely to go alone to new venues. Often they have to talk for a living and have to psyche themselves up first before each client. For these natives it is unbearable to be in a place that is not to their liking, their mind would be considering all too many things, like Sherlock Holmes, noticing all the little details because they have time to; because they are not being swept up by their interest in others. They aren't interested in everybody. They like people who share the same values. Mercury here is astute; New Taurus wakes them up to their physical surroundings. This Mercurial placement which was in its element in the Tropical Zodiac of just Gemini, here has more endurance, more focus for one subject but needs calmness to process it all.

It is not so much that these natives are shy as much as they are reserved; always. They are civil and tasteful. Their reservation does not preclude them popping in slight verbal ticklers as they get to know you. Neither one nor the other and both, this is Venus in Old Gemini; shy, cheeky, teasing, reserved. New Taurus here makes them appear friendly even when their tricky nature has made you unsure how to take them. The blessings bestowed by New Taurus on Old Gemini is that these are not fickle people; they know which side their bread is buttered and there is very little chance they would throw that away for something they can do freely in public; banter, flirt and tease. The beneficent planet of Venus likes to attract all that is good and in this case all that is good is someone who talks but does not bitch, someone who gets on with their roles and does not keep accounts and above all, someone whom after a lengthy period of time proves they like this Venus here. The apparent reservation shown by this Venus comes from stabilizing their perception of you (as they talk to you) 'knowing without knowing they knew'; which is their baseline for how far one can go in being cheeky or reserved with different people.

Mars in Gemini is so obviously showy about how they dealt with tricky situations and came out best, like Brer Rabbit. Despite the influence of New Taurus, Mars here is not chasing luxury but they do have hardiness about them, a pride in the strength of their body which, of course, they are inclined to tell you about. Where Mars is such a deep and egotistical animal, finesse cannot really be pretended. I would say Mars rarely shows finesse though it might delude itself in the old Air signs but really it ends up just pointing out its largess in words. Here we see Brer Rabbit nature coupled with strength. The stars of Taurus are focussed on strength, winning positions and the friendships of others that can help them. They flirt to sell something at a later date. After all, Taurus does care for business. Textbooks say that this placement jumps from one project to another though I have found many successful businessmen have this placement. They are not particularly competitive just self-motivated to have their bread buttered early so they can get on claiming, owning and winning. They do not want with their guts they want with their mind, they want something because they think it will top their show. That's their winning strategy; they don't care that much about *things* and that way they can keep a freedom to move around obstacles, take risks, bluff and above all *win* more things. Life is a game.

Jupiter was in its fall in Old Gemini of the Tropical zodiac because its abundance spilled out all over the place and seeds were scattered too thin. However, with the influence of Sidereal Taurus what tends to happen is that Jupiter here does too much for those in his inner circle; the neighbours, his siblings, mates, friends, children because they believe good fortune doesn't count if the others around you are not so fortunate. This Jupiter is easy to approach and if asked will nearly always say 'yes'. In terms of the higher mind aspect of Jupiter, this native is extraordinarily idealistic with a practical bent that is full of annoying realisms that can make them kinder to others than to themselves.

Saturn in Tropical Zodiac Gemini has always surprised me how enduring it is. It is not hindered when it comes to applying itself to dedicated and continued work. Looking at it from the perspective of Gemini, this can be the result of mentally understanding the need to persevere. They can reason and motivate themselves to commit years of time and energy to the practice of something and to be fair, Saturn in Tropical Zodiac Gemini does commit itself to the perseverance in not just one skill but more likely two or three. So how have the stars of Sidereal Taurus made a difference? Clearly it is the commitment, the endurance and determination to keep going at a particular practice. These people are some of the easiest to teach but also incredibly patient in teaching others, probably because they remember and know the feeling of dismay at the beginning of learning something new. They apply patience when learning another new skill.

OLD GEMINI/NEW GEMINI

Old Air - New Air

A blue djin blows into their bottle and creates itself.

The double Gemini combination is undoubtedly communicative. They commune with anyone about anything and if they can't – then clearly there is something wrong with that person! Communication to them is like the sense of touch is to the double Taureans. For the Ascendant here, talkative is beyond chatty. They see all the links from one idea to another, it's like their mind has no boundaries; it's all one world. It is like all the things that can be named share the same nerve. It is wonderful to watch them in action. Although their awareness of themselves may seem egocentric, it is really a central position from which to hook together more links. Through communicating they get a sense of presence and you may feel they talk too much, are they even listening?...they are indeed listening and logging new combinations of thoughts into their storehouse of 'ideas that go together.' They are sad when you end the conversation, unless it has been over an hour long, then they feel they have expressed themselves succinctly.

The Sun natures within these degrees are quite aware of their communicative skills and their ability to read between the lines; they make excellent salespeople. They don't mind being salespeople because it is not the product they are attached to. They are glad for the opportunity to be spontaneous and are naturally confident in weaving in and out of a conversation so it doesn't go stale; this gives them a sense of meaning. Their inner child nature is easily released in our western culture, so that these Gemini's have good mental health because it is easy for them to express and experience the brighter parts of their personality; spontaneous chit-chat. Their child-like nature gives them the freedom to go anywhere and talk within a variety of circles. For an Air sign, these Gemini's are the easiest to approach as they really do appreciate your ability to talk back and listen. The obviousness of the ordinary is fascinating to them.

Moons within this sector of the zodiac are imbued with the need to communicate. Some people need to feel physical comfort and some need excitement in order to feel that they are balanced in their soul. It's their norm. Double Gemini Moons enjoy the sense of being with their kin, and people of all ages. Perhaps it was these Gemini's who created the word kin; people who feel like family. Some may have blood ties and others may not, this Moon sees them all in the glow of 'kin'. You can see them as young adults getting ready to go out: in the bedroom are a group of mixed ages, aunts, cousins, siblings, toddlers and friends. These Moons relish and thrive in these situations. They feel especially connected when there are a variety of people around them.

Mercury here has an excellent mind as you would expect. They use it to get on in the world and they get on and stay within their own sphere. So when success from using their skilful tongue finds them, they stay close to their group. It is funny how Mercury in Double Gemini can go over the same banter with the same friends and each time it seems different. It has to do with the moment. They live in the moment when communicating, so each word, each gesture is charged with fascination. They find links between disparate subjects and seem to have a psychic knowledge in plucking out of the Air the subject that is particularly relevant to whom they are talking to. It is because they see all the little signs – they hear the *choice* of words – and the choice of words gives more clue as to where the speaker is coming from on any particular subject.

Venus here likes to be seen as easy to talk to. She likes to look young, think young and be young. From this desire can grow an immaturity that comes from not maturing. She can get stuck in looking in the mirror and forgetting to look within; not out of vanity but out of confusion. She can mistakenly believe it is her youthful looks which attracts them, then gets upset as she does get older. This placement can have a meltdown in their 50's when their looks have gone; but then they look within, find the elixir and are the classic young looking Gemini's. The stars inspire this Venus to gamble because they are very astute; they do tend to make good gamblers because they notice the signs others often miss. But they don't usually – unless there are other aspects – get addicted to gambling. Frivolous gambling may be a minor pleasure but their real joy is the gambling in business; on ideas, on people in the market.

Mars in Gemini really does want a rapport; he really does strive to share common ground and most often he does succeed. This Mars is best suited to writing; people can cause too many triggers and flashbacks with their issues. He cannot help but notice other people have so many issues. If he wrote it down it would at least clear most of the surf in his mind. But he is still likely to be provocative with his words. That is also what makes him quite fun to be around. This Mars makes an excellent detective or police officer or even a lawyer; anyone who needs to root out the truth not only with words but with actions. They like to put their thoughts into actions and see if things hold up.

Jupiter in double Gemini is a bit spaced out unless they find a mission bigger than themselves. They need to see the bigger picture without getting stuck on talking about it and just accept everyone has their own perspective. And after accepting everyone has their own perspective they are mind-blown processing how many people there are in this world. Jupiter in double Gemini likes to think whilst they are running and therefore enjoy marathon training around their town. They also enjoy walking groups for the chance to walk and talk. In fact, walk and talk is one of their favourite sayings because their mind relaxes when they are doing more than one thing at a time.

However, Saturn uses the walk and talk technique to save time and manage as many things as possible while conserving as much energy as possible. That is why these Saturn's do not seem particularly ponderous; the native lacks over-arching authority – instead they are like everyone's equal which is quite charming when they clearly know their skillset well. With Saturn here the native is glad to use their focus, on words naturally. Not using their Saturn nature makes them carpy and over critical – 'just saying' kind of people. But once their Saturn is in action they benefit the world with a hard copy of their thought processes and let others get on with what they are doing.

OLD CANCER/NEW GEMINI

Old Water – New Air

The sea reclaims some land and rejoices, sending up spray to the approving albatross.

In this Distinction the main trait that furthers the individual and humanity is nurturing. Whether you nurture an animal, plants, children or lovers, nurturing is a way of teaching and passing on your knowledge. The 3rd House which belongs to Gemini has always been known to be that of a teacher. Yet it isn't just teaching that goes side by side with nurturing a prodigy, it is also the ability to be equal to the student; the equality of the parent and the child. This is the placement of respect and modesty. Compassion for all beings and maintaining your dexterous mind also opens the gate to speaking with those close to you in ways that they can understand. Take nurturing to the nth degree to find communication with the motive to try to find that bridge; the bridge that enables discussions about feelings –feelings that can undermine you or the feelings that need to be nurtured because they are the feelings that will make you strong and kind. Mother and child, student and teacher; they are equals. This Distinction is filled with complex opposites that are really side by side.

The karmic knowledge of Tropical Cancer is to 'Love the one you're with'. Their intent is to look after the closest of their birth family, which is the family they grew up with, who will never be supplanted by their new marital family. Neither do their friends come into the first circle. Old Cancer is clear about their circles of closeness. New Gemini extends gentleness to a further circle of acquaintances. They are interested in many more people than was expected of Old Cancer; they are like a cool blue lake. They are open, unafraid of intimacy while being sensitive and careful with others. They are unspoilt. But consider the young people with this sign who can be snappy and scratchy with others; these have come from homes that were broken; it was as if their inner circle was broken. The poor child born under the stars of New Gemini that was treated disrespectfully and carelessly has had their heart centre broken like the clasp of a precious necklace and serious work needs to be done to thread the beads of trust so that they can be gentle again. It is this natives' desire to be gentle. They are not naturally aggressive because anger tears up their nervous system like a plough with blunt blades. Yet even the most wounded of these natives has a way of communicating with others that offers sincere interest; and there is nothing that anyone likes better than to be found worthy of gentleness.

Whenever I meet a Tropical Cancer Sun I am always pleasantly surprised at just how good at communication they are; they are sincere and earnest – but with gentleness as I said earlier – and so unselfconscious when they break the ice; that is such a gift. So the old stars have given these people the love and care of their intimate circle and the new stars have extended that circle to include neighbours, friends and marital relations and to communicate well. It seems old-fashioned - this centralized domestic placement in a world full of busy schedules and routines; they bring that sweet breath of simplicity. The natives of this time of the year know something precious about the ordinariness of life.

I would expect much the same for the Moon as what the Sun in this placement is inspired with but the truth is I have seen that old Cancer Moons are way more Cancer than Gemini. They are hooked on their intimate circle. They know their need to be with the people they are close with and stick with their few trusted friends. It is very hard for them to let go of what they feel secure with, they have no need to! Who would demand it of them? The new Gemini stars have less of an influence here; these natives do not like to leave the area where their mother lives and they know virtually everyone in the neighbourhood. They relish speaking about everyone – certainly not bitchily, though they tend to withhold information from people they are not keen on; there is a delicate balance of gossip and openness. Even a mother who is not favoured as much as most Tropical Cancer Moons favour their mothers is not treated to the withdrawal of information. Though perhaps the real gift offered by the new Gemini stars is the emotional intelligence as coined by an American psychiatrist from Oprah Winifred's show; these people know exactly what they feel and why they feel it. Perhaps the Sidereal stars of Gemini have opened up the mind and put a light into their emotional centre. They are inwardly reflecting people with a natural intuition that guides them to be clear about their feelings and also to know where their feelings stem from. The stars of Gemini make available a lot of environmental information which the old Cancerian Moon uses as balm to heal emotional bruises of those in their circle.

The intuitive nature of Mercury in old Cancer perhaps comes from the Sidereal Gemini which lights up thought processes and relates things emotionally. Rather similar to the Moon but then that isn't such a strange thing given that Cancer is so strongly related to the Moon and Mercury so strongly related to Gemini. So when Tropical Cancer is preceded with Sidereal Gemini the Moon and Mercury are as linked as one end of a type writer ribbon is linked to the other. It is known that this placement of Mercury gives a good memory and whether that is the Cancerian influence, like a mother duck who counts her ducklings without counting or Gemini which strengthens the

Mercury influence is unclear. I am inclined to think it is the latter, as the proof of the Sidereal zodiac and Tropical zodiac working together shows repeatedly to add benefit. Mercury in this part of the sky is also interested in its surroundings; it enjoys and finds thrilling all the little nuances that float in and out of consciousness like wafts of fresh Air awakening an animal's senses as it sniffs the Air but is never really threatened. So it is kind of instinctual and intuitive this Mercury, but curious, very curious, about its surroundings.

This is a lovely position for Venus: sociable and open on all sides yet airily light and floaty. The influence of New Gemini makes Venus not jealous despite its essence trailing from a Water sign. Though Venus feels vulnerable; they feel emotionally soft and compassionate, they know they won't want to hurt anything or anyone and this vulnerability serves to make them a peacemaker. You wouldn't find this Venus in a disruptive or explosive situation anyway. They can sense people's emotions quickly and succinctly. These Venus' are the friendly, charming people at parties who leave early and you miss them later. Perhaps they are rather too good to be true: they do not like intensity, they like easy-going, polite and pleasant surroundings. The women are sweet-natured, sweet looking, good girls, unless of course they aspect Uranus or Pluto. I think with this placement there is a real contentment of what their life is and how it is. Of the colours they choose to wear they like cool shades with a startle of jewellery or scarf or broach, something that mixes two styles together. They notice the little things and have many nik-naks that hold valuable memories. She is a mixture of femininity with dexterity; not strong or Earthy like her sisters, but soft and dreamy, quiet and gentle. She rows her own boat to the island to picnic with the rabbits. She walks like a cat and curls up with her lover. She likes new places but not alone or at night or anywhere dirty. Naturally, long mealtimes at a table with friends and family are one of their favourite pastimes; they accept other people's idiosyncrasies without a ruffle of feathers because they are especially polite but then, anyone who sits at their table has already been vetted.

Sure, Mars here is a protector of home, his castle; that is his karmic knowledge – to keep the sanctity of his castle yet neither is he such a domesticated lamb. This nature likes to eat and live comfortably but he strives to extend his boundaries to friends and especially neighbours. The new stars of Gemini have given old Cancer an eye for extra dominance in his realm. Mars here extends his energy to his immediate neighbours to be king of his palace and grounds. This position of Mars is not attacking in any way; it is defensive and would only attack as a means of defence which is learned from the stars of Cancer. This could make them rather tetchy or snappy but new Gemini has given them a reasoning mind and a desire to improve where they live. This Mars is helpful and kind, a bend over backwards type of person. There is a deep sexual desire nature too that stems from the bottom of the sea and spreads its influence like the light in a boat in the middle of the black sea under a black sky - the only distinguishing marks to separate sky and Water are the flickering swirls of luminous green plankton licking around the boat. Mars has created a haven in the midst of nowhere with only its inner-light as boundary.

Jupiter is considered in its exultation in Tropical Cancer because its influence of abundance is maximised into good feeling and positive values shared with the family so the good vibrations flow out; like in Buddhist meditation, from the centre of one's being to their family, and they in turn extend the positive vibration to their friends, and so on. The ancient astrologers knew too that families share astrological traits just as real as biological genetic traits, so Jupiter in Cancer shows that there are other positive vibrations in the home. New Gemini stars spread this influence further to its neighbours; generosity with friends, neighbours and teachers so that the native believes in the goodness of humanity. Everyone seems so kind. It comes as a revelation to see that compassion which comes from their essence, their inner openness, and unobstructed trust is responded to in kind.

Saturn learnt that family life is optimally safe. They maintain it within traditional structures to keep it safe; this is its innate wisdom. Saturn takes the Gemini stars influence as intellectual, because that is where Saturn is more comfortable as words help keep a distance. If the family structure is safe, words are kind. The sense of safety is shared with the environment and community. This placement of Saturn values education and skills and how to make use of the local environment to extend their security.

OLD CANCER/NEW CANCER

Old Water – New Water

The fountain bubbles up from the sea and flops back down again.

These Ascendants are wise. They know what they feel and what they are intuiting. Their shell is a little harder than their younger fellows – the Old Leo/New Cancer - and so they are not thrown from one feeling state to another without making a home in each feeling state. They don't hide their feelings at all from themselves and start building emotional roads back to their base feeling state from an early age. They aren't afraid of emotions. Disappointment from let-downs or excitement from a surprise is like travelling to other countries; they stay in hotels and head home to their usual feeling state asap. These double Cancers find the ordinary world very interesting just by being themselves. Every feeling state is of interest to them. So naturally, as they experience ups, downs and sideways feelings, they collect a repertoire of how people act with certain states of mind; which is why they understand where others are coming from.

With the Sun here the natives are solid about home. They aren't solid about much else but home is their mission. They cling to an old relationship till they realize the shrimp got up and left its shell years ago but loyalty is not the reason they cling. It's from necessity. To them home, family and security are so tied up there isn't much of them outside a home. It is these people who make the world go round; who give the street a 'safe-as-houses' name. For these people charity begins at home and their family are their life. Even so, they can create family from long standing friends if forced to; but the natives who have rough miserable families are wounded by that. So they stick around as long as they can, trying to fix the centre of their world.

The Moon at these six degrees is deeply emotional. They have such a deep emotional nature they can barely live with themselves – so they understand how others find them difficult! Their feelings shift and torment them with inner truths on a daily basis. These people need to process their emotions regularly; daily. Because although they have an emotional nature they too still need the few hours (at least) till the emotion becomes a clear realization. These Moons are kind of lonely too; they know no-one really understands where they are coming from and that is why they make such good companions. They are a comfort to others because they have accepted their aloneness and are quite independent about it. Most people say that Cancer Moons hate to be alone and cling; yes that may be the ones that haven't learnt the lesson but those that have, really do carry the world's soul. They literally feel like the mother to the mother of all beings and their responsibility makes them ache with love for everyone. That is why they are there all the time; watching and checking on you...their self-reliance is profound.

Mercury here is not quite as strong with their memory as the Old Cancer/New Gemini's; these Mercurial natives are far more interested in the domestic realities of their environment. They are interested in cooking and children's development. They like architecture and DIY. They are interested in the stories of their family, the family tree and best of all are the conversations at the beginning and at the end of the day around the table. They don't try to be clever and feel no need to make apology for their simple interests.

When Venus is in this Distinction the influence is one of abundance, plenty and beautiful children. This is the Queen of the hearth and she knows her realm. She is proud too of her place and what she has created and protected. This is a very feminine placement that gives credence to feminine rights and yet has the subtlety to encompass male initiatives. There is no hypocrisy here. It is a peaceful exchange of energies seen exactly for what they are. Above all it is comfortable; and that is the real gift here, that the native is comfortable between the male and female energies in their life, and does what is necessary to keep that easy exchange. Although the maternal archetype is strong in this Venus, so too is the fertile maiden; and when older the fertile maiden is expressed through tending gardens and dinner parties – whether in forests or snug houses.

Mars in double Cancer has a healthy admiration of female strengths. He wouldn't pick a fight with a woman, he knows their power. These Mars prefer to fight and challenge other males and that is to keep their own realm clear of any intruders or confusions. Mars in Cancer - old and new - makes sure their environment has space for self-expression; they hate to be crowded or be coerced. In keeping with their inner sense of coming from a strong place they retreat often to process the energies in their environment.

Jupiter at the Distinction of Old/New Cancer is again blessed with a sense of abundance and comfort. They are gentle, welcoming, home-loving beings who thrive at their own parties. Their family is extended to friends of all ages, genders and walks of life with the common denominator being a love of fun, relaxation and being themselves. They need nothing extra special around them but keep the philosophical outlook that the best kind of person is naturally themselves; so simple. And they strive for these qualities themselves, noticing any stresses and anxieties as not their own true nature. And if everyone is as they should be then the world is fine.

Saturn influenced by the Old/New stars of Cancer is however more stressed and anxious about the home being just right than whether people are right. They learn to trust their judgement and in old age they become the central authority of their family. They keep their family small and are careful to not include anyone until that someone has paid in time with their presence to the family. In the social world this Saturn respects and honours the work/life balance for everyone else too.

OLD LEO/NEW CANCER

Old Fire – New Water

The fireplace has been swept and the jar of pearls is open.

Pride and independence brings confidence and self-belief. These are wonderful traits; but like all the others if these traits do not transmute and change they would become arrogant and self-promoting. When the native brings their children and those they love into their inner world, they nurture them to taste their freedom from doubt then these constellations flow well together; like hot and cold Water in a river with a hot spring channel. The Cancerian trait of protecting the home and their immediate family also protects the Leo trait from burn out. This shows us that staying in and retreating is not just a timid thing but a way to blaze again. Equally, being afire with inspiration and dramatic display cannot continue for ever and needs to retreat and nurture itself, by nurturing those you love. The courageous blaze of Leo cannot blaze continuously. Like Fire uses up its' fuel Leo must retreat to blaze anew and this placement of Old Leo/New Cancer knows the value of those quiet times; knows the value of its' home and family and so they are truly loyal to their intimate circle; though their intimate circle doesn't share their limelight. If it did they would have nothing to recharge from.

With the stronger, dominant signs it is easier to see the differences that are the proof of Tropical and Sidereal astrology working together. Here, Leo's strong identity associated with being a 'Leo' lures them into keeping secret their own gentleness and desire to stay close to home. Leo's possessive and instinctive nature that comes out in times of necessity is where the new stars of Cancer have influenced this placement, for Cancer is possessive and protective of their home environment. Like Tropical Cancer they would protect the image of the mother with fierceness however, unlike Tropical Cancer they won't allow her to take over. In terms of family they feel special and like to get into their family tree and genealogy. Also noticeable with these natives is a pursuit of elegant surroundings to feel relaxed and be at home in, as in cafes with settees – it is these people who will always manage to get on the settees! They are subtle and it is this endearing influence on the otherwise boisterous leonine nature that makes this New Cancer/Old Leo modest with something to be modest about. They are not slackers or dawdlers, they go to work, work hard, come home and spend their time with family and close friends; they love the company of others whom they are close with and with whom they can shine. These natives can be scathing of people that do not deserve notoriety, fame or adulation but by some means they get it; because these natives pride themselves on working for it.

Where Sun in Old Leo/New Cancer was less showy than expected, here the Moon natures adores the limelight and is further bolstered by their family of how valuable, worthy and adorable they are. These Lunar natives totally expect and believe that they deserve all they want and will often presume and take up their position to receive what it is they want. It is true they may lack some of the modesty of the Sun in this position but that is because the Sun shines more conscious light onto situations, whereas the Moon is instinctive in its nature and just appears to take. However, when they are made aware of their presumption there is not a trace of uppityness, not a trace, and it is that pure innocence that is so very charming about these Moons; so you step back and offer what you had previously resented to give. Creating the loveliest home with all the creature comforts is important for them so they can give the pleasure to friends and family. These Moons like to cook three course meals of the most exquisite food; they do eat well but not as much as double Sagittarius, Taurus or Cancer because Old Leo is far more concerned with elegance and gluttony would assault their sense of being charming. The people born with this Moon have a certain something which makes them loveable; even without an easy Venus, these people have a loveliness that is comfortable to be around. Within their family, work or friends they command the centre. It is easy for this Old Leo/New Cancer Moon to step in and set about arranging an event to happen; though whether they actually organise the event is another matter, probably they will delegate – as they are equally capable of stepping out of a duty they do not feel is their cup of tea as they are of stepping right into something they fancy.

They cannot bear to criticize themselves so they are careful to have no need to. They are not morally devout like the Pope, or philosophical like Sagittarius but they are humanistic and intolerant of those who seem careless of manners. Mercury in Old Leo/New Cancer is interested in cooking and of being the best cook, with a large variety of cook books in the kitchen, where they should be, not on display in another room. The rest of their library is on display in the main part of the house as they like the look of the library as in theory again it adds elegance to their lives. New Cancer Mercury's have intuitive minds and are careful to not upset anyone, keeping personal thoughts to themselves unless in confidence. Cancer stars have made Old Leo much more careful towards others, and so Mercury, whose thoughts move like lightning, has plenty of time to appraise someone or the situation; they want to be known as having manners.

The Venus' of Old Leo/New Cancer are glorious creatures with a sparkle in their eye from the tender and modest influence of Cancer which creates a kind of excitement and alchemy of charm when this native flirts with you. Though they don't mean to flirt 'per se' it is just that with the complex influence on Venus they like everybody, because mostly everyone makes them feel the thrill. This Venus likes to be out and about and is keen to go places after work or in the lunchtime, this is probably the time that most of their money is spent. They like to look expensive but comfortable. This Venus can also be quite hurt by a snide remark – another indicator of the Sidereal stars' influence over the Tropical influence; quite sensitive to the opinion of others; Venus here likes to be petted and assured of their value; like a cat or a pet who needs plenty of physical stroking this one thrives on the emotional security of having its place assured within your heart. This Venus likes to be in the midst of fashion, with the Cancer influence of feeling safe in the middle and with the Leo influence of being their best; it results in clothes that are 'spot on'.

Mars, after all, is a warrior, not a man with slippers and a pipe; Mars is always a warrior; Mars is the warrior within each of us; our own Beowulf nature – tempered by constellations and aspects. Mars in Old Leo/New Cancer may have come out of the battlefield but he's not at home yet; this Mars is coming home with his mates. This Mars is celebrating the battles won. This is Beowulf after killing Grendel before the dragon is grown. The Leo Mars who takes great pride in their children is something that was always known about this placement but now Sidereal astrology shows this influence comes from the new stars of Cancer. As much as they enjoy celebrating with their family they need to win regular battles. They need to keep their edge and their maleness. They believe in human strength and they use it for those they love; Cancer has given Leo direction.

This is a bombastic Jupiter, kind to their family, generous with enormous appetites and prevalence for luxury. Though not as materialistic as Jupiter in Taurus, Jupiter in Old Leo likes decadence and is hedonistic as pleasures clothe their soul in the proof of their belief that they are fantastic. This might sound inordinately immodest but is it immodest to believe one is good, fantastic even, like in that song "I feel good! - I knew that I would now!" Isn't it great to feel so innately good! To have that self-belief and faith in yourself – and of course, remember the new stars of Cancer – in your children.

Saturn is happier with the Sidereal stars of Cancer than the Tropical zodiac of Leo as old Leo did not like limitation or authority. Old Leo was its own authority and that was the key to Saturn in Old Leo. Now, Cancer comes and softens that authoritarian and bossy nature. Saturn in Sidereal Cancer earns responsibility and willingly accepts it, though Leo taught them to not accept any other person in authority. Later hours at work, dutifully perfecting work and meeting deadlines to improve their position is a way of proving their own inner authority. They choose these limitations and duties. Saturn here has learnt the beauty of duty and so these successful and responsible people, after working their way up, deservedly get their wonderful family holidays in the Sun.

OLD LEO/NEW LEO

Old Fire – New Fire

The flaming nugget is bolstered by the other orange coals.

Like Taurus/Taurus, Leo/Leo natives are of fixed natures and believe that they are right and stick to their opinion or course of action in what is often interpreted as stubbornness but is also called strength of character. They have a very strong sense of self-belief. This is such a blessing; even the most severe aspects are tempered by the over-whelming sense of shining. Leo/Leo trusts its inner nature. They love life and love being with people; and who can blame them for enjoying and sharing their energy. Life looks simple for those born with their Ascendants amongst these stars; there is no need to manipulate, they see people in a way that make others respond well and their own natures are innately good.

When the Sun is in the corner of the old House of Leo where some of the stars of Leo still shine, there is the lesson to really trust, really believe in their solar nature and let it guide them; and to use inner strength to not get deflected and stick to their goals. To get to know the solar nature in its true and magnanimous essence so that what is good for them is good for others would mean deepening their faith in themselves and stepping into the world as their Self. Although this is what is required of all the Sun signs, with Leo there are no other drives. Again, rather like the Taurus/Taurus Moons; where those Moons might seem boring to others for just needing to be essentially Moon nature, the same is true for these Suns, to be just essentially Sun nature. The modesty of these Suns, or at least their lack of arrogance, is part of the good nature of this placement; it is as if their consciousness has been extended to be clear about their own motives and actions so that they work to maintain great integrity. The Sun proves its right to rule this realm when we can see how the natives are averse to ignoring their solar natures; it is as if the Sun has more power here. The Earth is furthest from the Sun in early July and perhaps these natives can sense the cyclical changes of the Sun, that by the time of their birthday the Earth is closing in on the Sun again and so they are particularly sensitive to the *effects* of solar energy.

These Moons relish attention; they love it, they deserve it, they have no shame. The Moon in Leo/Leo is very similar to the Old Leo/New Cancer Moon except they are more potent and intense, with fewer breaths for a bystander to catch before the next display. Of the entire zodiac I think these are most suited to the stage. There's none of that pining for solitude or fear of not living up to their image instead is a Moon nature that thrives on Fire with Fire; it could be anywhere; home, hotel, office, public transport, these natives are nourished by attention. I know that sounds that they could be like vampires living off the energy and feedback of others but that is the furthest from the truth. These Moons put in way more than they often get back; which helps to define their inner circle of intimacy. Naturally their closest confidantes will be equals – people who also put in more; Leo/Leo Moons are natural givers in attention. They walk into a room and their interest in you bathes you in the reality of your very own glamour; thrilled, you open up, you respond enthusiastically and they respond equally. They have a huge reservoir of enthusiasm and glamour most people pale beside them. So it's true these Moons are showy but they are also incredibly generous with their attention and it may be that the focus of attention is to find others with whom they can share a moment of celebration.

The old stars of Leo gave Mercury charm and the new stars of Leo just made sure these natives were the ones that spoke with confidence without severity and directness without bluntness. The verbal and sophisticated elegance of this placement comes from an education that is learnt in whatever surroundings they were born in; they are capable of mixing with the most educated people without feeling lost or looking foolish. The person born with Mercury here has good ears for listening, a dextrous tongue for the correct formulation of words at whichever speed is necessary and awareness of what is needed within a communicative situation.

When Venus is here these Leos are apt to be the most beautiful, made up fashion extras anyone can have in their box of friends. Joyfully they experiment from a young age – ooh what can I do with my body? And look how people respond! These Venus' are not shy but demure in a sultry sort of way as the Leonine joy has been given over to the desires of Venus. But the ache in these Venus' is that the world is not as cracked up as it should be, so the disappointment with the world adds a kind of charm and mystique that is not easy to read or please. They can be rather enigmatic. On one hand shallow and flirty, just into the show for the satisfaction of their desires and on the other side is their sense of value and not much can live up to their expectations. These are the modern artists who create some narrative on sex, using, in keeping with Leo, expensive means, such as velvet instead of sack, big galleries instead of empty shops, decadence instead of paucity.

Mars' pursuit for sex shows itself in fashion, fun and in sport and winning. We have a match here with other Mars natures who expect to win, such as Aries/Aries. This Mars enters in to the competition with the burning drive for the results. It isn't so much the game itself but the winning at the end of it, so they do what is needed to give them the best chance of winning, whether research or press-ups, Mars in Leo/Leo is focused on the end product. This doesn't make them a bad sportsperson, they are not deluded to think they can win everything, and they will play kids and let the kids win – sometimes – but they are wilful and ambitious to get what they want at the end of it. I think this is from Mars as the 'henchman' of the Sun; Leo has shown Mars to give precedence to the solar nature, whichever constellation the Sun is in. So this is the legacy of Old Leo – to know that its Will is subverted to the solar nature – to all that is bright, true and good in ourselves; and then they abandon self-consciousness and go for it.

Here Jupiter brims with confidence and generosity. It believes in itself, it believes in all that is good, right is on its side and Law comes to mind for the expression of its beliefs; equally so does religion, in a fervent and passionate way, as Jupiter is that part of us which strives for bigger and better things, who sees there is more to life than ordinariness. Lush and abundant ideals surround this Jupiter and it is up to the native to put their visions into practice. Perhaps the glorious vision is too grand to make real and this Jupiter strives and strives to make more and bring more into their lives. There is a touch of materialism here but it is only the reflection of divinity.

This Saturn works so hard and tries its absolute best. It goes by the rules because the rules make sense; the rules reflect virtues and virtues are the way forward when the black sea sips at the beaches of the mind. There was never any doubt this Saturn would work hard and long hours to achieve its aim yet it is the spirit of it that throws light on the native. Civility is honoured where it should be and where it must be, but should anyone act rudely or unnecessarily stupidly, then this native will openly and directly chastise. Here though Saturn lacks the self-belief of the Sun, for which it is the shadow. Yet what is remarkable, is the duty in which this native will continue to do the right, moralistic, virtuous thing; in the absence of light (the Sun) the rules are followed and Leo dictates that the rules guide us to virtue to feel and be good.

OLD VIRGO/NEW LEO

Old Earth – New Fire

The Earth spews magma and more of itself is created, in its own image.

Meticulous focus taken to its nth degree brings joy; needless, exuberant joy for the sake of joy; that is the power of concentration. Of course all the gurus and Buddhist monks know this as a fact like the knees bend after a jump, this faculty of mind is obvious to anyone who knows about focus and concentration. Neither of these signs seek out meditation, unless in the 'intuitive Houses', though this Distinction inspires fascination with numbers or letters or some other ordering system. This gives them the love and attention to focus for a period of time on their interest. So you can imagine someone really getting into whatever they do with this placement; accounts or singing, cleaning the church floor or hairstyling; these people focus and do their best work and when they are done, woo! They snap a funky song grooving across the work floor. Then they get into their focus again....

I was always surprised by the outgoing and creative nature of Tropical Virgo before I discovered Sidereal Astrology but now it is clear that the old Virgo stars are influenced by the very outgoing Leo stars. The karmic knowledge of Virgo, to organise and prepare has been given an added boost by Leo to dare and to give it a go. Leo has given Virgo the confidence to take a shy look around and gage their skill and prowess by the talents of others. I say shy because not even shameless Leo could give Virgo the full confidence to look around at the work of others and dare be totally immodest. So here, Virgo has gained in confidence to look around and gage their worth and their worrying is really the Leo drive to stay on top.

Many, many times I have seen artists with a Tropical Virgo Sun and it seems that these natives are drawn to modern art with their predilection for perfection – the perfection to create their cleverness into – most often – sculpture. Although I say their cleverness, it is really my clumsiness in finding the right and appropriate word for what they "hit upon", because this Old Virgo/New Leo is in no way romantic or idealistic; they do not consider their visions to be paramount nor intellect to be the be all and end all - though they are far closer to accepting intellect as the precursor to great art than vision or inspiration. To be fair, the innate knowledge of Virgo has probably instilled in them the value of physically doing something and in the doing of something they then "hit upon" the right form for their art. Old Virgo has bestowed trust in the physical realm and New Leo adds creativity and flair. I also noticed the outgoing nature of these children and considered, here in the west, it is because the school year begins with people born on 1st September; so of all the class these are the oldest children of the class year and hence expect to be one of the best. Perhaps the structure of our school system is stronger than the constellations or it is just coincidence that the oldest children are in fact showered with the blessings of the stars of Sidereal Leo? The integrity of the solar nature is matured through effort and order, the traits of Virgo past, yet Leo gives something so natural and golden it almost slips away and gets taken for granted; that is their natural belief and trust in themselves that they can make things happen.

They say the Moon in Virgo worries and that must be the Moon that is in Old Virgo/New Leo because it is something known in astrology nowadays. It is said that it is a typical Virgo trait to worry, picking at loopholes and presumptions, almost irritating itself and not letting things be. But I have seen this Moon would be far more irritated if it did not do what was needed to do in order to have the peace and order it craves. In fact, this Moon, when at home and at the height of its powers really knows how to relax. It relaxes in a big and dramatic way. There is the known kindness towards guests serving them the very things they like and in the way they like it, which stems from the Virgo nature but the added Leo influence is to include light and warmth. Beautiful lights, extra warmth, this is how Old Virgo/New Leo works together. But once these Moons sit down to relax in their heady Leo atmosphere within the realm of Earth they are unlikely to disturb their own peace if they can help it yet often enough it is just the little things that if they were done would add to the perfection, so they jump up, complete one more task, proving the influence of Leo is spontaneity – just do it! Get it done! And whilst the Old Virgo Moons knows exactly what is needed to make a perfect environment to relax in, they have the added Leo influence to make things 'the best' now.

Mercury is happy in Virgo and Leo adds to its speed. Mercury here is known for their direct, dry and caustic tongue. They see too much, know too much, little eludes them and they cannot hide behind a halo of light; it is the very light of Leo that has given them greater consciousness in all the things around them, helping them put it all together, which makes these Mercury natures rather judgemental. They have put things in order, in boxes and you can hardly be surprised when they roll their eyes when someone gets it all mixed up. These Virgos want to be the best; like the Sun in Virgo of the Tropical zodiac Leo has bestowed the confidence to look up and look around so these old Virgos know they are mentally a cut sharper and more diligent than average and with Leo stars here they are more keen to let it show; 'just saying'.

Virgo Venus' like Leo Venus have both been renowned for their preference for decorum and traditional values – for their distaste in what is vulgar, rough, ready and raw; both too are known for their passion, it is the finishing touches of this genuine value that causes desire. So I cannot decide where is the dividing line between Virgo and Leo in the passionate nature that demands proper etiquette but I can show that the Sidereal stars of Leo have influenced this Venus to be a more showy girl, rather than the demure and modest nature expected; however Venus here knows that to be demure and modest is attractive and uses this as part of its show.

Modern man; here it is; macho and sexy, confidently expressing the practical and domestic side. Mars here is concerned with getting down to the nitty gritty and Leo rewards it with the praise; of which, incidentally, this Mars enjoys but does not expect, rather it finds it funny that something so simple and easy to do is given praise. It laps up praise but is not a lapdog. Mars always has its own Will, its own way of doing things and here Virgo has given Mars a thoroughness that compliments its determination. All Mars natures are wilful and determined; where Virgo makes this Mars thorough, Leo makes this Mars confident; it believes in itself and is inspired to show itself, reveal its skills; that is why this Mars is so often in responsible positions; it can do the job, knows what it can do and does it in a way that gets noticed. This is the position of sexy accountant or bank clerk; what was once considered staid and boring has been given a new patina of sex appeal.

For Jupiter in Virgo there was a tendency to squander its hopes and idealisms in petty irrelevancies but with Leo covering the scene Jupiter can breathe more easily. The Tropical Virgo trait of painstaking scrutiny is uplifted by New Leo. New Leo has added glamour to the scientific mind with young, intelligent people looking cool without ties and in reputable careers. Science is fun; lining up objects is art and the stock exchange is a stylish place to be.

Saturn in Virgo adds detail to work and with perseverance strives to bring order out of the chaos of the natural world. Here Saturn is repaid. New Leo, whose stars have been shining where Virgo used to for many years now, shows the influence of Leo accepting its human authority and has brought humanity closer to usurping God through science.

OLD VIRGO/NEW VIRGO

Old Earth – New Earth

Kerching! Kerching! Coins roll in. Joyful physical sound.

Old Virgo/New Virgo is not some neurotic or perfectionist itching around trying to make the world perfect; they are calmer than that. They see everyone has a part and that is why they feel such great respect for every being. Everything is just about to spring into action, just about to be perfect, just about to happen, which make these Virgo's like a host half an hour before the party starts. Everything is prepared, 'ok, calm down' they tell themselves, 'breathe...' and then they focus on what needs to be done now. They are neither mean nor extravagant but perfectly focused on necessity. This sense of order brings great peace and internal comfort. They offer the first guests refreshments immediately, ask if they like the music; they lavish their first guest with attention that in the world away from Virgo/Virgo the later revellers do without. Everyone is the first guest with these Ascendants. Other people's carelessness or even messiness does not bother them as they can accept other people have their own priorities; unless this Ascendant has to share their space.

Old Virgo/New Virgo Sun keeps their own counsel, though no-one would say they are secretive just clear about what the next thing to be done is. They don't mess around as there is always something to do. Even fun is like an exercise, as they mentally tell themselves, 'now is the time to relax...' These people don't come out into the field much. They like to stay at home in the evenings to prepare for the next day. Whatever job they have they take it seriously, they don't think anything is beneath them but they do have preferences to do the job they are most suited to do. They know their own limitations and their skills too, so for them it's virtually painful to do something that is beneath their skill level because of the waste of resources; unless of course there is nowhere to go and no way to climb any corporate ladder, in which case they do their absolute best and wait for an opening. If their talents and skills were being wasted their integrity inspires them to move on, and leave the wasteful company. Another trait of these Suns is law abiding duty. Again, the waste of destruction sickens them; the thought of unhygienic prison conditions deters them and the thought of forgery just sends their inner thoughts amok at the chaos of disorder. These wise Suns were born to take the shortest route to get to where they want to go and for them the journey looks straightforward - a beautiful unfolding of necessity.

Moon within these degrees is particularly body orientated. They make excellent parents or nannies. Routine and order keeps their homes safe; they like to be able to read or write in peace; by a lamp – to not waste light but shine it only on the words needed; in a clean room. If they are surrounded by mess they cannot enjoy reading, or writing. They write journals, lists of things to do, shopping lists, lists of dreams, lists of passwords. These Earthy Moons are also very aligned to pagan practices. You will find more pagans here as their soul hovers above the boundary of the autumn equinox; they sense the bounty and the mystery with every breath. The Goddess in all her forms resonates with the Moon in Virgo.

Mercury sitting in Old Virgo/New Virgo is a writer. They put their words down. They manifest their speech. They materialize words. They edit and prepare useful words such as policies and speeches. Somehow they find a way to concretize speech and equally they keep their sentences brief. Clarity and brevity is promoted by Mercury in this placement.

When Venus is within these few degrees the native is influenced to maintain purity and simplicity. Naturalness is beautiful to them; uncoloured toenails, au-natural make-up and pure food ingredients in and out. These Venus' love being close to the Earth, clothed in the seasons is when they feel beautiful and what they value in others too. They are healers of all kinds; helping people to align with their innate energy, trusting to nature to restore the balance of optimum health. Health is beauty. The New Virgo brings spiritual awareness to the care of their physical chariot. Beauty is not their object; functionality is. They like to show their natural health. Ripeness and blooming lovely is how they feel and what they value the most to want to express.

With Mars in Old Virgo/New Virgo the native does things their own way. The Marsian energy is by nature a lone fighter and when in these few degrees they save time doing what needs to be done themselves - if it is worth doing. They do not delegate carelessly. Their to do list must be ticked off every night and they cannot be bothered explaining all the details, as by the time they have found the right person for the job and explained it all, the thing that needed doing could have been ticked off. In terms of dress, they like to look robust and healthy, strong and fit and so typically, in our modern world, the gym calls them.

Jupiter brings stoicism to a new level here. They can almost appear fanatical the way they love the old philosophers. These people search for truth in the everyday and ordinary times. Health again is a matter for concern and is marked by the zest to do the small things, such as tidy and cook. Jupiter exalts robustness and therefore lets of steam through exercise; because if they didn't tire themselves out every day then this Jupiter gets frustrated and ironically more tired. Their body is part of a bigger picture and to be connected with the greater plan they need to be as healthy and as fit as they can be.

This is a happily placed Saturn. It works hard and doesn't feel bad about not playing. It strives to create a vocation out of whatever job they do so they can carry on working till they drop. They ensure they don't waste their time; time is their companion. This Saturn is naturally very successful in the material world as even from a young age they planned their career. They planned everything.

OLD LIBRA/NEW VIRGO

Old Air – New Earth

"Don't just talk about it – sort it!" Hollow boxes, hallowed taxes; the landscape changes the horizon.

When you take the principle of Libra to its extreme – that of fairness, diplomacy and peacefulness you see it becoming further aware of even more nuances; because every case, every scenario or situation or person is different. With this combination the truth of the moment is strengthened. Everything is constantly in flux. There is no situation that will be exactly like the last; so Old Libra becomes concerned and even more aware of the eternal changing moment and with the wisdom of the enlightened beings they tread very carefully. You have to tread carefully when you see that the moment is like putty to your own ideas. Diplomacy and sharing ideas with the motive of creating a more peaceful world naturally leads to analysing situations with a fine toothed comb. Old Libra is aware of the duty they assume to create a peaceful environment and Virgo honours that duty and determines to be clear about things that are difficult to clarify.

Methodical, punctual and conscientiousness from Virgo mixed with the tactful and gentle nature of Libra creates a character that is not doubtful of their probable perfection; and they are modest too – at least modest enough to appear modest! As an Ascendant these stars make a friendly person who is particularly careful not to upset anyone for no reason but should anyone be unreasonable this friend would pick up on it and without fuss or show take the most civil course to have nothing more to do with them.

This Sun that we all know as Libra has peaceful and tactful character traits; but they are Virgo. Although reluctant to prolong any argument they are not a push over and will stand their ground in an invisible sort of way. They enjoy finding the right course of action and will not interfere with others though their solar natures are like a bright light shining on the walls of their threshold, like prison guards, they are acutely aware of who's in or out. Frivolity is something that may have happened in the past, it's OK for children but now necessity and duty become the focus for the meticulous Virgo. They never really let themselves go; for instance, slobbing about in pyjamas is just not their scene unless the pyjamas are ironed silk and the dressing gown gorgeous with matching slippers; if they wore a lounge suit it would be smart enough to go out in and though they know others relax in this way, they do not; if they did they would be depressed, such is their nature to maintain an outer decorum which enhances their sense of order. They have mental boxes to separate fun and non-result orientated goals and only when Virgo can file spending times with friends as a necessity will they down tools and spend an evening having a pleasant time. They are cool and easy company, because by the time they have come out to play there are no other pressing duties to attend to. They prefer fun and easy times to work and routines but Virgo has also given them a desire to complete their work and routines; without which they feel lost. So they work hard and maintain a peaceful mind of meaningfulness despite their work. They have the biggest work ethic in the zodiac.

For a Moon they are distant from their emotional needs because they tend not to feel things intensely; everything is OK, it is 'cool', they can work their way around most situations. Yet they need order and a sensible amount of food to feel peaceful. Peacefulness is the natural state of their Moon nature. There is a sense of harmony in the environment that these Moons need and expect so they can slip away from the world and feel peaceful. They will gladly do some work to create their nice environment; but not dirty, heavy work. They like eye-contact too, but not intense like a Scorpio; eye-contact helps to keep them from flying off into a fairy flight of irrelevancies; which is always their secret getaway door as they don't want to get bogged down in any subject or tied up with any passions or obsessions and they will only take on commitments when they are absolutely sure. It is also noticeable that these Moons are not bitchy and cannot bear bitchiness; they are very kind and sweet people. Bitchiness falls away from their ears like the last petals in autumn; there is no sound, no big to-do just the obvious letting go of awkward company. Virgo gives Libra Moons more concern for the health of their body, that it is not just good for appearances. They are protective of their physical threshold, their skin, as they are of their psychic threshold and would rather be alone than be in company that made them feel even the slightest discomfort. They get up and leave as easily as a waft of air goes out through the crack in a door.

Mercury comes alive with this placement; you could almost say Mercury is in its own element, though Mercury has no elemental abode, being the spirit that moves between all elements but here Mercury is inspired by Virgo to penetrate the issue further. I think this is why Tropical Libra Sun was always considered to make excellent lawyers, because a Libra Sun would in a third of the cases have a Libra Mercury. They are great talkers and debaters and they need a calm and orderly environment to think straight. Virgo enhances the Libran debate to pinpoint their winning strategy.

Where Virgo is polite and likes to please, physically, Libra is charismatically elusive; Venus in Tropical Libra is known for its tangible pleasantness. Virgo adds attention to detail, like the eyebrow plucking, hair styled, make-up applied like a professional, clothes matched; these are all clearly the work of the stars of Virgo. Though Venus does not burn with a passion in this placement, Venus has a drive to accept what comes her way. Its nature is to attract what it wants, so Venus here treats everything that comes her way with care and respect which in turn elicits the best response in others. This may be why Venus works so well with Saturn here, because as these natives get older you can really see the power of Venus in action; the calm and careful, attractive power of Venus is personified in an elegant older woman who is perfectly manicured and makes everyone around her feel treasured, without sexuality, without sentimentalism but with a smooth Airy dignity. Classiness and clothes are part of their esteem too; they prefer plain, elegant styles, unfussy and far from glitzy. Rich and classic fabrics have proven themselves as being worthy of being close to their skin as they cannot bear discomfort.

Mars in this position takes on much of the rest of the chart; it is not that it is weak but dutiful to the Self. Virgo adds to Mars seriousness - to get things right - and Libra is content to do its duty. Mars overall is well-mannered and cultured using books, letters and social media as their domain. They will stand up for what they believe in; they make good lecturers, being not too forceful but clear about what they mean.

With Jupiter the old stars of Libra encouraged high and sophisticated ideals whereas Virgo urged this influence to research the past and present masters in their field; just to make sure. This Jupiter has an excellent memory because they are thrilled and excited by books, knowledge and accessible philosophy; Virgo makes the accessibility and usefulness of the knowledge an ideal to keep striving for so this Jupiter is often keen to keep studying.

With Saturn the surroundings are kept clear of the debris of sentimentalism, fluffy ideas and impractical left overs; this is a practical environment in which the stars of Virgo have pushed the old stars of Libra to create. They support the traditional structures and through rules, contracts and written warnings Saturn here affects its power. Virgo and Libra support the nature of Saturn and Saturn likes the environment Virgo and Libra create. Duty and work are enjoyed for its own sake.

OLD LIBRA/NEW LIBRA

Old Air – New Air

Through the tubes of transformation, green gas becomes yellow gas, then clear.

There is something substantially peachy about the Old Librans. They know exactly how to make themselves seem peachy, though they are not fakers. They display peachiness because anything less would 1) draw unnecessary attention to themselves. (They don't mind attention when glory is due but attention in the form of 'what's wrong? Or 'you seem out of sorts, what's up?' are considered wasted and possibly harmful for future unknown reasons. It is better to be safe than sorry. Old Librans are careful so that nothing will come up and bite them on the bum.) And 2) detract others from talking about themselves and share their best story. Libra/Libra Ascendants find everyone so interesting and they love judging all the phrases, styles and gestures. Of course it has occurred to them that if the judged were to focus on the Libran they would in fact feel agitated, even though the Libran has already judged themselves they do not need another to do that for them. Old Librans are on a spectrum of awareness of this hypocrisy but that does not deter them. They are very generous in their openness of letting others judge them but they do their best to not leave a shred to find.

The Old Libra/New Libra Ascendants are expert at looking traditional without looking staid. Perhaps the word 'perfect' is better than 'traditional'. As it is not the past structures of society they honour but the classic styles that have always worked. Their aim for perfection in expression is a philosophy that minimizes cracks and moments of confusion or doubt from others thereby increasing the peace in the world at any one time. If this native is deemed *avant garde* it is in a way that is impersonal like a painting on the wall. And this native is careful to ensure that their life-painting is seen in a gallery. They are contextual licensees but there is nothing shallow about them at all. Instead they are complex and deep; too elusive to say; obviously cultured.

When the Sun is in the segment of sky ruling Old Libra/New Libra we find integrity is paramount; integrity that is disinclined to draw attention to their integrity too. They judge themselves, morning, noon and night; measuring their character as they age till they conclude to say less about their reasons. Never complain but always explain – if asked. That is how they learn to be. They hold themselves together in the freedom of the silence around them and honour their environment which gives them space. These Suns are happy being unconcerned about happiness. Happiness or sadness is just another mind game because no-one can take away their inner thoughts.

With the Moon in Old/New Libra the native is a bit confused in the modern world because they don't really want to touch it and they don't long for any hard working good old days where they would have worked close to the Earth or scrubbed sore fingers in soap suds. The modern world is full of abstract excitement but Moon in Libra wants nothing; wants for nothing and knows it. They do not want to get involved or bogged down. They create their own simple environment that is clean and friendly with space to think and silence to listen to and that's it, they are content. This is their ideal but typically the ideal is impossible so these Moons retreat often or their teeth start to clench.

With Mercury at these degrees you have someone who likes to speak up for silence, space and the right to live one way or another. However, in order to make their point they need to explain their case. They are expert at giving reasonable reasons. In order to win their argument they excel at debate, listening to other arguments and weighing the facts; though they really have already decided so their fact finding process is weighted and then they just pick out everything they need to prove their point.

Venus here is positively lovely and loveable. Serene and untouchably beautiful, she floats in and waves a blissful scent to bring peace to all those around her. She isn't looking for glory but if eyes were to be dismissive or critical she feels ill at ease. Nothing horrible can exist in her world. This Venus keeps up appearances as if continuously manifesting peace in her own environment. As she gets older her world become smaller because the world and his wife are so uncouth. She settles in her world with fewer people who can disturb her. This Venus has the sign 'do not disturb' on her door always. That doesn't mean she is unhelpful or unapproachable – in fact her approachability – when you have good reason - is one of her charms but please don't be unnecessary; please be conscious. She won't hang around if you have a disturbing nature.

When Mars is here the native is keener to debate and bring order to the world. They like bureaucracy for the order and equality it offers. They are proud cogs in the relentless wheel; they are individually proud of their ability to keep systems running smoothly and their skills at ironing out troubles. These Mars do well in the world. They get promotions and deserve high positions as they are neither greedy nor egotistical. Pure Libran energy is like the good cook who maintains the right temperature and is careful to add just enough quality ingredients at the right time so the delicious food isn't too rich or heavy but easily digestible. They just don't get on people's nerves.

With Jupiter in this position of the zodiac you have a very beneficent person in authority. Mercy and kindness are their ideals and they do all they can in whatever position they are in. They are happy to give second and third and umpteen chances. They believe in an individual's power to change - to recourse and navigate their life for greater harmony within the environment - and they believe it is our nature to not want to harm or upset others. Perhaps they are optimistically idealistic but they, unlike the Venus here, still maintain a wide circle of acquaintances to have an influence in.

When Saturn is in this part of the zodiac the native is determined to uphold any structures and traditions that keep the peace. Prison guards and police officers up to chairmen and leaders of bigger organization are typical of jobs they value. This Saturn has its place in the world and takes its place. They are neither too critical nor harsh though Saturn here has a strong influence, and the native feels this like a sense of destiny - they need to respond to these calls. This is a socially responsible Saturn.

OLD SCORPIO/NEW LIBRA

Old Water – New Air

Rebirth through the hole at the base of the pyramid; breathe the modern Air.

The principle here is that of passing judgement; finalizing the matter and dictating the odds. Old Scorpio sees what needs to happen now for the process of advancement. Scorpio weeds out what no longer has any place; Scorpio gets rid of the dead leaves. New Libra is revealed by the following-through process. When the old has been identified someone has to assert that. Scorpio identifies the old and snips all the brown bits off and this trait changes into the awareness of judging carefully. This is a decidedly merciful inspiration. In the bible of Scorpio all that is unnecessary needs be weeded out; all that is on its way out is hurried out the door. With Scorpio, change is welcomed. Change is sought. There is no need to cling to outmoded behaviours – or people - yet Libra brings in conscientiousness and respectful consideration of what the next expression will be like; Libra likes to keep some of the traditions. Without the breaking of the wave the Water just gathers and climbs higher – it has to reach its end point and burst into its new form. The energy that inspires us to change takes time over the process; it's not a fierce cutting process but a molecule by molecule event to a new world order.

This Ascendant can be represented by having a steaming Turkish bath in the North of England then stepping out into cool Air. The toxins have gone; here is a renewed spirit, ready to take on the same old battles without getting embroiled in dirty fights. You might think this Ascendant shouldn't be afraid of anything, since it's been to its depths and knows in its heart what it is to yearn and thrash about with temper and despair but now the stars of Libra, so civil and so calm, so careful not to jump to conclusions or let their own desires get in the way, offers a sense of peace, that this Ascendant is almost afraid of breaking its own spell. They tend to have a tight grip on their passions while letting their desires guide them. They create a path through life that little pieces of energy can seep through in small doses, so as not to upset any apple carts.

The old Scorpio Suns are less obsessed about certain outcomes as Libra has shown them the power of staying calm. By not being too passionate one way or another is not a compromise of their desires. They have learnt to put themselves in a position where either outcome would benefit them, so they have to be flexible and they have to be ready. However, the Sun has just moved from a fixed state so they have to be more accepting of change and find a solid sense of centre from which to act from. These Suns are not too attached to groups; they like to be independent and private, that way they can safe-guard their inner soft belly and move with less baggage from one situation to another. Both Scorpio and Libra work together to maintain the privacy of the individual; Libra teaches to not spill out all over the place as it considers such behaviours uncouth and Scorpio never has any intentions of showing anyone their weaknesses. In their private circle of friends and family they are more expressive of their preferences but still careful not to go in like a bull-dozer; their way is one of calm determination. It is the new stars of Libra that have helped Scorpio release and let go of things; Scorpio by itself would just brood and cling even in a black hole. Libra has given Scorpio the name of the rejuvenator as Libra helps Scorpio move on to the new thing, leaving resentments and bitterness behind.

The Moon too is helped by the New Air of Libra. Without Libra this Moon would cling to any old past feelings and needs; Libra brings the imagined relief of what it feels like without those heavy feelings. It's like this Moon has had a head start in psychology, it is close to its own unconscious patterns and the spirit of Libra is like the sky sitting on the surface of the Water, looking down, contemplating and not getting sucked in. This Moon is a mixture of passionate precision and intense calmness, watching their own depths; fascinating and fascinated. Yet they don't trust much; probably their own images don't coincide with what is happening so they are constantly working to bring their inner understanding in line with what is happening outside of their bodies. When there is nothing to be fascinated by, that's when they feel life is boring. They have an insatiable desire to be mesmerized and awed, though, being sharp eyed, they are not that easy to charm.

Mercury has a good understanding of whom is motivating whom, what the crux of a problem is plus some good ideas as to why; yet it keeps its ideas safe until more information has been found. This Mercury can slip in and around many views, perspectives and mental blockages that it can appear manipulative; but it is only finding out more information. Mercury, wherever it is placed can listen and feedback what is needed or what they want you to hear. Perhaps this Mercury is manipulative; their realm is people and relationships, so naturally they have a lot of information from just watching and listening.

With Venus the Scorpio nature is relieved by Libra and can get more of her desires through using the polite and gentle aura that is traditionally modest and inoffensive. The Scorpio nature knows her desires and finds them automatically fulfilled by using the charming Libra Venus. This Venus is inclined to find a fashion that doesn't reveal too much about them. In this sector of the sky Venus wires us to things that have space around them; like lone trees in the night, like small animals out alone, watching. Not lonely or neglected people but people who hold themselves or part of themselves back so they don't show fear is an interest for Venus; it magnetizes her. Libra guiding Venus in Scorpio makes this introverted nature slow to capture her love interest because it is possible things are not what they seem; so she waits and watches. Intensity builds; just the way Scorpio likes it and Libran nature flows in and accepts her prize or floats out as if she was never there.

This Scorpio Mars attacks and retreats with terrifying eyes but the noticeable thing about Sidereal Libra is the politeness and acceptable measures it will use. Libra has affected their mannerisms that these Mars can be mistaken for mild and very ordinary but like their Venus counterparts it is the way of molten rock on the inside with a cool crispy shell; fascinating and alluring. They do not step outside the norms of social behaviour. They are held fast inside by a guiding morality inspired by the stars of Libra; though they can walk with stealth and storm like a God through a door. Those born with Mars in this sector know their own body, its limits, strengths, weaknesses as well. It's why they can dare so much with certainty and that quiet certainty is part of the charisma of Mars here.

Jupiter is full of fertilized seed in Scorpio; there are many options available that will nourish its desires. Libra thins out the seedlings; Libra gives each thing space. There is an abundance of care and attention from the ancient fascinated eyes of Scorpio. For each object of interest it gives space for it to grow as much as it can. Open to new ideas, this Jupiter can express its hopes that have matured from childhood. The long-held beliefs of this position were created from the unspoken scraps and lost broken links found in the past; they won't let go of them easily because they have such belief an ideal world will come back to life.

With Saturn here there is perseverance and determination to work hard, and a fear of failure which pushes the native on to achieve its goals. It doesn't take on many goals; it senses the need to achieve one goal at least, like wind eroding rock, and won't waste its energy spreading itself thin. Libra is a sharp judge and critic here. The defensiveness of Old Scorpio melds nicely with Saturn and Libra adds a veneer of manners to hide itself better. This is a very dignified Saturn.

OLD SCORPIO/NEW SCORPIO

Old Water – New Water

Topping up the bath Water to remain in for longer improves the purification process.

The essence of Scorpio is preserved for longer because the usefulness of knowing where the juice is between people is a great survival mechanism. When Planets and Angles fall within these 6 degrees the native has a reliable sixth sense. When the Ascendant is pointing to these degrees the native is deep within themselves. They know what they are looking for or waiting for. They are like hunters for the energy they follow. The energy is an emotional link between themselves and others; a trail, a scent, a definite and – to them - palpable presence. And whoever has this scent becomes their guide. However, from the outside it could be that whoever has this scent becomes their prey – but the fact that these scorpions humble themselves to their guide is part of their bewitching and entangling process. They are mesmerizing, captivating and magnetic to the person that shares the emotional energy link because they are in turn mesmerized and captivated by them.

When the Sun is within the degrees of Old/New Scorpio magnetism is again present but the integrity of the Sun nature ensures that they use their power for the benefit of what is real. So many people think Scorpios are bad natured and greedy for sex but they are far more drawn to the emotional energy of connection. Unlike the other Water signs though they don't want to be seen as needing others, so they are defensive yet vulnerable. It is because they are vulnerable and afraid of being shunned they are so hyper-alert to the emotional connection with others; many Scorpio Suns say they know whom their next lover is the moment they meet them. These Suns are acutely aware of their own individuality; of coming into this world alone and going out alone. And along this journey they seek special emotional connections - which they treasure - and that is the crux of these Suns.

With the Moons the native is far more vulnerable, defensive and spiky yet loyal to the emotional connections they do make. They too treasure intimacy, knowing it doesn't come often and it doesn't come easily; intimacy is special. Another lasting lesson from the old stars of Scorpio is that they carry their own baggage; they don't project their fears or desires, so they are very straight forward in that respect. They also believe anyone can change; people are like a flux of emotional phases and although they know this about themselves they also know they cling to past emotional connections and so accept the very human traits of clinging and possessiveness in themselves and in others. The time to let go always comes, eventually ...

Mercury at these few degrees is, as you would expect, particularly astute and aware of the emotional environment. They are like gangsters in a dangerous environment, or old foxes that are alert to the snapping of twigs and the fake smiles of snitches. And they are extraordinarily careful of other people's feelings, which may look like compassion; carefulness of other people's feelings is pure sensibility. It makes sense to keep others in their place, not stir them up unnecessarily or shock or agitate them, because when others are troubled they start effecting the environment, maybe even causing this native a headache with their whining. That is why this astute Mercury keeps the peace in a subtle and controlling way.

When Venus is at this corner of the zodiac there is no other lover than the one they have that special juicy connection with. This Venus will not bother with possible lovers and wait for the connection to grow or for attraction to build. It is either there or not. This special connection used to bother this Venus as she is aware of the emotional juice between others as well yet no-one talked about it. She can feel the emotional entanglements and intimacy being shared in auras; but now this Venus has learnt that not everyone acts on these feelings. She is stronger for knowing this feeling and wiser from realizing that not everyone even attunes to it. This very feeling gives her attractiveness in her own eyes and that is what matters to her.

Now Mars in the Old/New Scorpio has the strength of Mars in Aries but it is subterranean; it is unspoken. It shines in the knowing look they sometimes give. These Mars hold on to that sexual magnetism and perfect it with even greater subtlety and disguise it behind suave manners. They are double agents, secret service spies; no-one gets to know their motives; only their boss – "and they is their own boss"[3]. However, these natives do not put sex top of their list. It is just useful, like a tool, a socially useful tool. A strong Mars does not take all the glory from the native Sun; a strong Mars works for the benefit of their realm and so Mars in Old/New Scorpio can have many types of motives but it is important to say they are less likely to be narcissistic because they know their own power and don't need anyone else's obedience.

Jupiter at this corner of the zodiac is hopeful and has that excited feeling that things just keep getting better. They have an optimism based on their sense of excitement which is intense. They care more for others than things and their need to be connected with a bigger picture gets merged with emotional connections – these Jupiters are often psychic.

---

[3]My mum – spoken like a gangster.

When Saturn is here the native has an iron-strong discipline and control over themselves. At best they do not try and control others but they will influence others because they are often successful and inspiring; though they are the strong silent type. Others see their success and their steady resilience yet there is no deal made out of it. In true scorpionic style this disciplined nature is hidden and smooth, and doesn't cause any waves on the surface.

OLD SAGITTARIUS/NEW SCORPIO

Old Fire - New Water

Transference so the fish doesn't die before the delicacy is cooked.

The qualities of exuberance, energetic faith and optimism are transmuted at the end of its line into making deadlines. You cannot go on and on expecting goodwill and energy to have no stop button. That would be exhausting for everyone. There has to come a time when you say, 'well prove it.' New Scorpio takes the bible of Sagittarius and twists the finishing touches. This energy manifests what was promised. The quality of optimism would be stupidity if there was repetitive hoping and believing in a new day; and so at the end of optimism there needs to come a time to be counted. Equally, exuberance exhausts itself if it doesn't retreat and brood over the events set in motion. Everything subject to time has a tipping point; new Scorpio makes that point when enough is enough and the changes that were promised are completed before your eyes.

This Ascendant gets surprised by their sudden outbursts of feeling, for films, for stories with beautiful endings; they have to learn how to accept this part of themselves. The spontaneous and outgoing Sagittarian nature is kept in check by the silent and passive emotional nature of Scorpio. Scorpio helps them to realize a sense of seriousness and dignity is not only what they deserve but desire. This Ascendant is incredibly sensitive; Scorpio has made it sensitive and Sagittarius keeps getting into situations most won't tread, so it gets ample opportunity to experience the deeper and darker side.

Scorpio depths affect these Suns. Sagittarians are known in astrology to get depressed because some find it hard to accept their 'other side'. Sagittarius Suns present as children that were valued for their good nature and optimistic outlook. Fire and Water are opposites and to unite them is not always easy but a healthy Sagittarian Sun is exuberant and boisterous plus it is deep and reflecting; Scorpio agrees with its philosophical search for ultimate truth, as truth brings power.

The Moon we know in Sagittarius is clearly not as cheerful as one would suspect; it is careful. It is as if it knows exuberance can lead to accidents so it is cautious. Though not at all morose, this Moon is moody and this moodiness infects their actions in Scorpio style; with a watching and withdrawn nature. Sagittarian Moons can be knocked into depression; I have heard it said that their ideal world breaks down and they are filled with disappointment, yet I believe this is another clear example of Sidereal astrology. Jolliness is their first natural state of mind so when these people go deeper than the layer of their moods they go under the sea as it were, where there is very little current, and here they become transfixed as all sorts of feelings blob up and pass them by. Unprepared Sagittarius can flap about a bit under Water but Scorpio nature is content watching these symbols, these objects of fascinations. This person lives with laughter interspersed with tears, a joke in the middle of communion, and a good hypnotic trance that gets deeper when it is returned to. Here the Scorpio stars influence an object of fascination with their own unconscious feelings and Sagittarians have to find ways to accept these deeper amorphous feelings.

This is an excellent placement for Mercury; it has speed, curiosity and the daring of Sagittarius coupled with intensity for truth from Scorpio. It likes a joke and will definitely make the most of the axiom 'many a true word is spoken in jest' which they use to their advantage, and enjoyment! It is hard to pin down this shadow of a butterfly because the imagination takes flight here. Imaginative, enthusiastic and magnetic they attract helpers to their cause easily.

Venus in old Sagittarius has a huge appetite for the good things in life and the person with this Venus takes in and gives back much joy. The stars of Sagittarius have infused this Venus with an attraction for lots of laughter with a wicked sense of humour. She is also lusty and flirtatious; all the Scorpio things in a daring Sagittarian shell. The difficulty again with this Venus, the same as the Sun and Moon is that Sagittarius finds it hard to accept its darker nature; the Sagittarian nature is so good natured and fun, and is often the star of the party that the darker Scorpio nature has to do plenty of self-development to accept their natural other side. These natures are nearly opposed but together they give depth of character. Yes, their melancholy and disappointment with the world is not much fun but their innate sense of fun can laugh even in the most despairing situations.

The rather lovely energy of Mars in Sagittarius/Scorpio evokes the image of the stag in the dark forest. He is strong, powerful and free, he is also private, which adds to the allure. This is a happy Mars; the person doesn't easily get confused about what they are aiming for because this energy is more direct. Scorpio helps that directness too with its seriousness and focus and teaches it not to squander its energy. Most Sagittarians do not go blindly ahead they only seem to, when in fact they have already looked ahead and weighed the possibilities. What this nature has is a strong faith in their own physical abilities; if they can imagine it then it can be done. The Scorpio stars inspire this Mars with great self-preservation, which serves to strengthen this Mars' belief that they will be OK. Although this is a good natured Mars a stag can do a lot of damage; they are protected by a cloak of dark leaves and not many would take on this formidable beast so they tend to be allowed to get on and do what they want, even with hard aspects.

Jupiter is exuberant here – of course; these people are not small minded; they believe in themselves, in big things, in better things. Their future looks good. Though Scorpio does have an influence here; it is that 'I've got a secret' way about them. Scorpio has taught them not to spill out all over the place and to hold back, keep some of what they thought of back; it adds to their sense of strength. There is an unquenchable desire for travel and thirst for knowledge but there is also a high drive for power, for strength, for being top dog.

What is unattained serves as a buffer against depression. There is a lot to be had and a lot to be done to get it and this Saturn is willing to keep working into the future to attain it. Saturn by itself in Sagittarius would have marked its own card successful as it ticked off achievement after achievement but with Scorpio here the fear of not getting the power and recognition they deserve pushes them on even further. The Scorpio influence through Saturn strengthens Saturn in Sagittarius and is an influence to keep going for their future.

OLD SAGITTARIUS/NEW SAGITTARIUS

Old Fire – New Fire

Emblazoned with a grand vision of cosmic support there is deep faith.

The Galactic Centre is within these degrees; it is a source of great energy. The energy from the centre of our universe inspires a constant supply of enthusiasm; a yes-can-do attitude. This Ascendant is of such a good nature most people don't even guess they are Sagittarius. They don't get up any one's nose, they don't start fights over slights and they don't blame or victimize anyone. They are steadfast in standing back – which is why people don't often guess Sagittarius – because although they are ready to engage their Fire and fast twitch muscles at a moment's notice they stand back so much because they like people. They accept the differences and the idiosyncrasies that annoy so many others. However, they are very competitive. Given any chance for a challenge they are the first to the start; 'game on!' they yell. They have excellent sportsmanship. Of course this all sounds like they are the most perfect and balanced people – who would want any other Ascendant – and certainly I think these are great Ascendants – but you must see they live their lives in this perpetual soup of energy – gathering and exploding in the moment. They need a goal as a constant. There is a strong connection with being part of a bigger picture; they need to understand and relate to a bigger picture.

These Suns need a goal bigger than themselves to feel connected; to feel vibrant. And that goal must hold great meaning. For this they use their reason, they add everything up and take away all that is unnecessary. It is not that the others aren't pure philosophers but these degrees love philosophy and use reason to understand their place in the universe. Their goal, above all in their life must be worthy. A Sagittarius Sun without a worthy goal is a knight without a king and a quest - a raider, a traveller, a tinker. They may have the charm and the sparkle in a wink that wins strangers to their aid but in their heart, nothing adds up; they feel a fake. Sun in Old Sagittarius/New Sagittarius have sagacious spirit. The bright wisdom of Sagittarius is in the moment, picking up trails and snippets and binds all the separate clues into one skein to create a bigger picture and a grander meaning. That is how Sagittarius Suns join the dots; from the inside. Their independence and bravery to face the truth strings all their findings like a trail behind the arrow and their love of others shoots that arrow out of the sky away from pettiness, towards a better goal.

The Moon in Sagittarius carries all of these qualities - she is like an actress in her dressing room. This Moon knows what the public wants but to herself she is real; she knows what she is playing, and so, more often than not she is even more likeable than the Suns in Old and New Sagittarius. In her dream she says she never wants to go on stage again; she would always be an out-of-work actress – if she could only earn money from her dressing room. That way this Moon is never compromised. Never having to act nice, not having to say the right thing in the right way or add the charm like seasoning to the moment – that would be her dream; staying behind the scenes and being accepted for whom she is. Moon in Sagittarius is driven, compelled even, to find out whom she really is; who the actor is behind the stage; and so this Moon is more likely than most to search religious and philosophical tenets to find their inner truth. To them there is no greater meaning than finding out who they really are; searching for the truth hidden in their hearts is their path.

When Mercury is coloured by Old/New Sagittarius you get someone who is thinking other things as they talk. Yet unlike their duplicitous opposites – Old/New Gemini – their thinking is more like a conceptual linking of ideas with other ideas. They see the wider scenario and hold it all in their mind's eye, placing the people with their words like pawns for killer moves. The world is a pattern of order hidden in a Sudoku grid. So as they get older they see more of the story, understand more; that is why they have so much to say and to share. They talk a lot to check out their findings. And when older and wiser this Mercury decides not to upset the world so they keep a lot back too.

Old and New Sagittarius' Venus is a likeable, loveable being and they know it. Both women and men with this placement are particularly aware of their independence and how that quality is attractive to them too. They feel their aloneness not as a punishment but as the realization of a blessing and see the aloneness of others too. Unity for this Venus is built on a mutual respect of independence and trust. That is not to say they don't get jealous. Jealousy is not beneath them, because they have strong animal instincts. They don't expect treachery but if it appears that way then they can be quite the dragon. They won't play cool just to have an upper hand. Their emotions are quick and on the surface but if they are cool, and they do walk away without a fight it wasn't because they were beaten, it was because they sussed the traitor out and disgusted they threw the crumbs away. Then they are free and their freedom is their most valuable treasure.

When Mars is in the place of Old/New Sagittarius the competitive animal nature is accentuated. But still they are good sportsmen. 'Best of both worlds' is their motto, as inner and outer play out through their actions. They are brave too, as you would expect – and certainly they want to be seen as brave – better brave than winning under false pretences. These Mars' natures need a goal, they need a king. They are not as independent as their Sun counterparts but they are loyal to their own native Suns. Which is how Mars should be – not running the show; not a hit man with ideas of his own; but the knight carrying out the will of their King.

Jupiter in the place of Old/New Sagittarius is as you can imagine; incredibly lucky. They reach for peanuts and they get brazils. They fall flat but get up seeing the path to a new door. They know they have the capacity to find new ways but thinks everyone does. They don't see that their own awareness of the bigger picture in the moment and joining the dots to find a new trail is their own ever hopeful, don't stop looking nature. This then is a clear lesson for us all; being hopeful and piecing together what we know is an on-going strategy to open new doors. This Jupiter is a guide. You need energy to carry out all these brilliant opportunities you keep finding.

Saturn would be this Jupiter's partner if each Distinction was a whole. Saturn in Old/New Sagittarius says don't waste your energy on this or that. Discernment is the key with this Saturn. Not out of fear but out of conservation of time and energy. This Saturn looks ahead, sees not everything can be done and keeping the goal in mind they plot an excellent, straight forward course. Again what matters here is the goal; if there isn't a goal then this Saturn just conserves energy and tries very little. Their fear might be to look up beyond the everyday material world and see nothing but more materialism but once they do look up, and once they allow themselves to dream bigger they have a good captain for their ship.

OLD CAPRICORN/NEW SAGITTARIUS

Old Earth – New Fire

Across the moors there's an orange window of light; a flaming hearth in a trustworthy bothy.

The principles that Old Capricorn personify are steadiness, continuity and maintenance. Left to their own wave of pushing on, depletion sets in; these energies become hard, rigid and brittle; but with the vibration of Sagittarius governing this trait we get a second wind. This second wind brings a gust of hope and enthusiasm; like when the goal is in sight. When you continue day after day, whatever the goal is, over time you will achieve something. Sagittarius energy comes in and reveals what achievements have been made and what is within its sights. The native is inspired to bask in that glory. There is renewed faith and willingness to adjust their course to keep the wind in their sails. It is as if the universe shows us through the bible of Capricorn that there will also come a time, after you have pushed on relentlessly, that you must adjust your course in order to maintain momentum to reach the greater goal.

New Sagittarius takes on its cardinal mantle with enthusiasm and totally believes its way is right. That is because the caution and deliberation of Capricorn is now coupled with a religious zeal for spontaneity (opportunities for spontaneity which are planned for without having to put up with sudden or extreme changes of direction). Earth and Fire, being alchemically opposed yet in need of connecting, offers the chance to put spirit into dull situations. What's nice about this Ascendant, despite them being absolutely sure they are right when they reach a philosophical conclusion, is you don't need to shout them down to make them change their mind; though their vision for understanding the world is engraved in stone. They hate to be seen as gruff old Saturnine types, like their very being knows it is not their true nature, they add careful bursts of colour to their clothes as well as explore new tastes and ways from other countries in a polite way.

You must have noticed with the Suns in this position that these natives are much keener to be seen as having fun and being seen as spontaneous as if spontaneity itself were a goal; sometimes they even refuse to make a plan. They say things like, 'when I make plans everything always goes wrong.' Sagittarius seems so much more acceptable than the ways of Capricorn as if the stars of Sagittarius themselves have no patience with the values of old Capricorn. The Capricorn nature shows itself in their stable lifestyles; their stability is protected and maintained by the very roots of society. The innate Capricorn nature would never let their stability be rocked. They have a desire for a lot of sleep but are able to keep going on unknown reserves of energy. Another similarity with their Sidereal sign is that these old Capricorns are fair minded and sporty, though they may not have time to relax they make time for outdoors sport and this can be contrasted with Tropical Sagittarians who are only presumed to be sporty while most are especially keen to luxuriate and philosophize. Not only does sport interest these Old Capricorn Suns but religion does too; especially fringe religions. The old Capricorn Sun has taken on Sagittarian clowning and silly funny behaviour - it is obvious that the stars of Sagittarius rule this part of the sky! It is often said that the Capricorn Sun is old when they are young and young when they are old; another pointer to the truth of Sidereal astrology, because their sensible planning and building a sensible future from when they are young is the gift of

Sagittarian stars that got this soul to look ahead and have a vision to make come real.

The same principle applies to the Moon as it does to the Sun in this position, and that is that spontaneity is valued and aimed for in a way that only a hard edged Earth sign can do; in a deliberate and controlling way they insist on doing things on the spur of the moment. It is as if they need to define their structures as unchanging and wide enough to accept irregular events. They like to cook when they please – could be 10 at night and lunch at 4 in the afternoon. They may like to cook with whatever is in the cupboards but the truth is they have stored for months. They may suddenly go to a Zen temple – but they have envisioned it for months. This Moon is also determinedly independent; yet this Sagittarian trait goes hand in hand with the Capricorn detriment of the Moon; determined to be independent for the fear of being let down triggers the anxiety of having to trust anyone less reliable than themselves; their prized independence is the very key to their freedom, and this Moon craves freedom from their own limitations. Funny childish behaviours are treasured as easy ways out of their loneliest moments; and children love this adult Moon because they know this Moon will skip down the street with them.

This is a heavy position for Mercury; Capricorn makes it slow and deliberate and Sagittarius makes it cast its net wide. Mercury in this sector of the zodiac loves long and deep conversations, where a subject is relayed by many experiences and the wider implications are teased into view. They find small talk a chore and would rather be silent though philosophical discussions at a bus-stop can be enjoyable. Mercury here is a good thinking mind who likes to break the heavy conversation – which they brought on – with cathartic releases of laughter. Unlike the Moon and the Sun here, Mercury can be more naturally spontaneous (but it isn't beneath them to plan many conversations in advance) though their quickness of mind tends to come in sudden bursts rather than being a constant while their slowness and ability to focus is probably more useful.

Venus in Old Capricorn kind of sums up the poor image of these natives as being rather prudish in public but often you can see the Sagittarian influence gives these people a hearty laugh and jolliness – but only where they feel safe. They can act like Saturn is on their Venus in places or with people that put them on edge; displaying perfect manners and not giving an inch when their hackles are raised. Sagittarius makes this Venus keen on going to the gym, white-water rafting and safaris. They live to travel, explore and get out of their rut; which they love to go back to after.

Surely everyone has noticed what a competitive show-off this Mars is! Yet they are also the strong-silent type; that's why they don't get a name for being macho, though you wouldn't think this Mars lacked anything in that respect. Mars here is ultra-competitive yet holds himself back from many challenges, appearing placid when in fact he is always up for the challenge. Mars here doesn't like to be the first to throw his gauntlet down; that's why he holds himself back, stores up energy, watches and is ready to pounce. He needs to use up his energy or he gets stressed because he doesn't like to take the lead yet there wouldn't be a winning team without him.

The Jupiter energy is inspired by Capricorn to check its boundaries, get up and look around, check on the outside, the blind side, till Sagittarius kicks in and there is a confidence and boisterousness precisely because they know everything is safe, and just how it should be. Capricorn does not encourage this Jupiter nature to make leaps of faith, rather to gamble with knowledge and keep the odds as low as possible. These are the people who work hard all their life and travel when they retire; they planned for it.

Saturn can be a stuck-in-the-mud warrior here. Left to their own devices they struggle with everything; they work to keep themselves trim, they work for their pensions, they do everything for a future and work so hard for a future they barely live in the moment and at the same time they wouldn't want it any other way.

OLD CAPRICORN/NEW CAPRICORN

Old Earth – New Earth

They could live on any planet beneath a giant dome to protect them.

There is a doubling of Earth and of cardinality that one cannot fail to notice; very little impress these people, and if it does impress them their 'wows!' are polite. They don't make any sudden movements but may just stand there grinning from ear to ear. They can accept most things, and for a long time; they can endure. And though their smile might fade they don't give up; their desire for life is so strong - if depression came upon them they react with duty because they are geared to survive whatever the cost. When faced with a fiery nature, they just nod as if they understand; with a hysterical person, they just soak it up and move on. Like a fox that sees the shed where the chicken is, they dig, dig, dig, every day, they don't see it as an obstruction, every day they dig, dig, dig, dig. There is no sense of 'woe, poor is me', unless they dug under 100 sheds and got no chickens. It isn't optimism that keeps them going; it's necessity.

This shy Sun is not confident in any situation; they live by the precept 'insecurity is where it's at.' The truth of this saying is deep and bestows a character that is open and new in every situation. Strangely, fearful Capricorns are the bravest of the zodiac. They count on nothing; from past to future, they play at life like kids with sand-castles on the beach, tirelessly bucketing out the Water. They are brave and live in the moment; geared to making that moment last. What matters to them are the sand-castles of their whole life; the physical world they have created; they aren't silly, it's kind of funny, making something last and exist. Their Sun shines best when building something from scratch that by their efforts are improved. They are excellent business builders though not like an entrepreneur; their business would be far more practical, utilizing specific skills, then all that matters is they put in 18 hours a day. They don't even have to believe in the business; just a practical, workable plan – point them in the right direction, and that's the way they go until it succeeds. Double Capricorn Suns have immense stamina but where they are drained is in situations they should have let die years ago. Naturally it is not optimism in trying and trying for a situation to work; it's a dogged belief in their own willingness to survive, they presume others feel the same and so any situation can be accepted. Neither does this Sun like being alone; they are always alone but they don't mind that; it adds inner responsibility, which adds strength; physically though, they like the *presence* of others.

The Moon here is equally vulnerable and knows how to protect itself with fierce capabilities and independence. The world of Titus Groan pales beneath this Moon. They have no mood swings just a constant desire to keep going but they understand and allow others the privilege of moodiness so long as they learn soon enough not to bother this Moon with their tantrums. Their motto must be 'good health, good life', as their health enables them to keep going though they do not do specific things for health; they just have no needs to do anything that might give them ill-health. To them, death is just the opposite of life and if you are alive you keep trying. They are all too aware of death that life is a dream and yet they keep going.

The nerves of this Mercury can get quite frayed, from the incompetence of others and the fact that they have to try and get on with incompetent people; most people are incompetent compared to this Mercury. They thrive on keeping address books and notebooks with dates. They keep a more pronounced order than the double Virgo because they cannot bear things being left undone. For their own peace of mind they tie up all loose ends and take the bins out before they are full though there is really very little stress in these natives if they can keep things together. They are never far from their duty – life is a wonderful duty.

Venus is not sure if she can finish something and if she can't finish it she won't allow herself to have fun, so she works from a deep reservoir of energy. They prefer work arenas to parties, as in the work space they come alive in glamour and classic styles, showing off their slim figures as it is unusual this Venus is overwhelmed by food or luxury. Instead, the richest things in life are reason enough to curtail desires and this is why this Venus lives so long; all things in moderation. Sex is not a luxury but a necessity; there is time for everything, from hairstyling to plucking and shaving; beauty and pleasure are attended to with calmness; the silent, wordless joy of traditions adds to the sense of presence of these natives in any company.

Gone is the showy competitiveness but now is the intense devotion to the success of a project. Mars in this corner is determined to build something to honour the aeons of Capricorn stars. They don't build sand-castles with their kids; they make drywalls and deep moats lined with pcbblcs. And the rampart is built further up the beach too. Their sense of caution and fore planning is to make their project succeed. They stick to traditional methods and only through their own skill and triple checks would they consider a better way or a new way, which it definitely would be. These Mars natures are strong and enduring; they uphold traditional values through their actions and choose sports that are lonely like marathon running; it is the same how they move through life; they want to win but not for the sake of winning but for attaining the goal.

Jupiter would be stifled but for its irrepressible exuberance which Capricorn channels into work and enjoyment within work and duties. Like Venus was happier in the work place, Jupiter is content striving towards the top of the mountain. They have flair and charm within traditional settings and tend to be the best in their field of what they do because they enjoy it so much and are happy to work long and hard at it.

Saturn though is over-worked here. Saturn has become somewhat hard and cynical. The triple Saturn influence is good for a successful outcome for a goal but they rarely let up on themselves. They do not sing or dance or prop up the bar with stories for everyone; they are quiet and sincere; deep thinkers, serious workers. Without the success they believe they have earned they become even more cynical though they try harder. Their stamina for their own projects is admirable.

OLD AQUARIUS/NEW CAPRICORN

Old Air – New Earth

The future whispers around the buildings of the new planet; like wind eroding rocks, like spirit breaking up hierarchies.

The principle of Aquarius goes something like this; all people deserve equality and equality means we are all entitled to have a good life. A good life isn't just for the bourgeoisie. But left to its own energy stream Aquarius just goes on and on saying the same thing, making the same points. They are the wind with no sail. Capricorn however is the manifestation of structure. The tipping point again is, 'let's make this happen'. And the way that things happen in this corner of the zodiac is through structures, rules, red tape and traditions. This is the energy that addresses the petition. It is no good having 10000 signatures and no-one to whom the matter is addressed. The tipping point of energy finalizes the energy; and in this case it takes appropriate action through the main structures of society.

These Ascendants are distinctly more traditional than they want to let on. They value the Aquarian ideal of freedom for the individual yet they try to pinpoint freedom or hold it down. They stand up for humanitarian rights and make rules that become part of the social structure. They get good jobs because they work well in modern fields of technology and within corporate structures. The old fixed Aquarian nature comes into contact with the enduring and Earthy Capricorn and so this Ascendant is not particularly sentimental yet capable of little, surprising niceties. They like making small modifications and consider themselves useful; they have a mind that is capable of genius marketing, modifications to technology or something that would make the world a better place; though not particularly interactive, more concerned with their own thoughts or ideas, especially with others on the same wavelength; these people are at the forefront of progressive teams.

The Sun here is not as bothered about the humanitarian aspect as you would expect; they are more concerned with their status and value hard-work; because with good status they understand they can do more to help people. They are careful to not give away power to people who are lazy or undeserving. If asked to help they bring help in an established form rather than perennially feeding the underdog directly. In their hearts they want people to be strong enough to help themselves and they are more concerned that their help may weaken someone in need; having fought so hard to overcome their own disadvantages they take pride in their positions of authority, though they are not authoritarian, just distant. In the silence of their room they work continuously towards concretizing ideas, no time is wasted; parties are opportunities to hear feedback or find new ideas to work on. Capricorn is helping Aquarius by making ideas real. Aquarius, with the influence of Capricorn, values society and civilization; it does indeed believe in a better world of equality for the basics of life but the Sun here is also very ambitious; partly because they understand the modern world and think they are the right person for the job and partly because they are more than prepared to work within the structure to fine-tune it.

Capricorn makes this Moon more modest and less inclined to fly away and be completely displaced. Home isn't easy for this Moon so its sanctuary tends to be the workplace; though Aquarius helps the Capricorn nature to settle in the house after a hard day's work because chances are they have all the mod cons and other techy comforts. Sometimes it is like they refuse to give themselves what they need or to admit to their own needs as they feel that needing something is a sign of weakness; even if it is a positive thing, like the need for an office job if they have Reynaud's Syndrome or their need to be ambitious if they are a mother of young children. They have a need to not be vulnerable, which is why they work hard and rush around tending to children and all the other chores too. Independence is a need that makes them feel strong and nourished.

Old ideas of new world systems are reconsidered in the light of how society can bring them to fruition; maybe there are new structures to establish or old ideas revamped for contemporary times. Aquarius is an astrologer and Capricorn is a mathematician; together there is a sense of genius and of proving amazing things through discipline. The stock-exchange is also highlighted by this position; no-one fully understands how the money goes round but this Mercury can have a better idea than most.

These Venus people are down to Earth in a non-practical way. They see things the way they are; imbalanced, unfair, complex and irregular; and their answer to the universe is 'respect'. Aquarius wants to explore, accept and attract everything, while Capricorn believes everything can have its use; so all the doors are open and everything comes to this Venus in Old Aquarius/New Capricorn. The stars of Capricorn, like the fat bough of an ancient mulberry tree reaches right down to the ground for anyone to climb on. Then they make plans to make things easier but become more embroiled; when then cut their hair so it is easier to manage they have a full set of high-lights which need re-doing every 6 weeks. When they buy 'sensible' flat shoes they buy metallic green ones that can't be worn in the rain. If they plan to go out after work they do all the work they need so they can leave early only to end up taking more work on because they have the time. This Venus is known to be enigmatic to the opposite sex; I think they are exceptionally friendly and accept everyone's differences.

Many worldly interests attract, spur and inspire this Mars and left to its own devices they may sit fiddling with an idea for years; Capricorn pushes it to make something useful. They are fair-minded to the point of stupidity in sport but have far-reaching judgement in other realms. They are not endowed with the killer instinct; mainly they don't need it, they find better ways of getting what they want. In business they don't let others win; they are able to differentiate between the structures of a business, of a game, of a plan, whatever; different pursuits require different strategies which Mars with the New Aquarian influence relishes finding and Mars in New Capricorn makes practical strategies with its innate wisdom of playing by the rules; it wins friends, companions, and people onto their side. This Mars gets people to work together.

Aquarius influenced Jupiter to be generous and kind so these people are often doing something to help people less fortunate than themselves. Perhaps as mentors or helping kids to read, their help is practical and strengthening. Capricorn uses the good vibes of Jupiter as a career direction with the idealism that where work and pleasure come together there is more chance of success. Also Capricorn helps to concretize Jupiter's big ideas; ideas which are for the Aquarian version of the betterment of humanity.

This is the very best position for Saturn sitting high in the sky; influenced by both its rulers in equal measure. Saturn is open to new methods and tries to integrate the new with old structures. Saturn can easily scythe what doesn't work or is no longer necessary. The candles are burning and it is for prophets to see in this light between tradition and the new; they look for the ending of what is outmoded and useless, to drop like stalks and fall to the ground then the Aquarian ideals poke through the stubble to become the new tradition.

OLD AQUARIUS/NEW AQUARIUS

Old Air – New Air

A bird flew out the open window and is still flying.

This Ascendant is similar to the previous Ascendant; Old Aquarius/New Capricorn but they are not so keen on being alone. They have a large circle of friends whom they are linked with through work and like-minded individuals who would be interested in one of their many projects or groups. They also enjoy people who are very different to themselves too and pets are a source of remembering the differences but equalities of others. They are especially good with gadgets and will have things such as recording key-rings, the top mobile phones and pens with torches at the end. Clothes are appreciated for their advanced appropriateness for our modern world; such as waterproofs and technical running shoes.

New Aquarius with Old Aquarius tastes the mystery associated with the New Age. These Sun signs are very aware of society and what the modern world has to offer. Double Aquarius Sun signs are careful to not interfere; or careful to not be seen as interfering. They are always checking their stance in relation to things happening in their life and though they navigate through not taking sides amongst people and friends they can get swept up by an ideal and become part of a movement or group for the betterment for society. Aquarius/Aquarius Suns look to be in tune with the time, whatever age they are; and though they try not to interfere nor cause fractions in their personal life they are not martyrs, so when they must draw boundaries they do so with an attitude so subtle and open that only the effect is noticed and no-one can really remember who started it. Another trait of people born with their Sun at this time is that they have an unbending faith in universal laws. They totally have faith that what is right becomes right, that what will be will be and that if something could it probably will happen so they back the side of progress, of the universe and of things much bigger than themselves.

The Moon in this position gets swept up with the tide of the time. The Moon is genuinely nourished by others with the same interests and who think the same kind of thoughts; it doesn't matter what kind of person, their age or their status, this Moon feels a rapport when others act out their ideals. This Moon is keenly aware when someone is living the way they find meaningful; and if you can find meaning in it this Moon will recognize it and be nourished by someone else who lives from the inside out. Being such a globally aware person makes individual contentment lower on its to-do list and Aquarius/Aquarius Moon is not so fussed about its physical or emotional comfort; this is why they are considered distant. They know too much about others and will never really be content if they had all the creature comforts and others didn't, so they don't chase this or yearn for emotional security; they have a comfort in themselves at not being too comfortable; it makes them closer to all the other people on the planet and that is where they truly feel grounded and connected.

This is a mathematical and analytical Mercury. This Mercury is fast and speeding around the heavens looking to piece together questions and answers that seem to be floating about unconnected in every conversation or whimsical idea. They talk fast and their mouths dry with all the Air that enters. They communicate in whatever way they can, looking for facts and others of like-minded interests, though they may seem like loners as there aren't many quite like them; very individual and original thinkers, they make a hobby out of thinking things through and are clear on many subjects, especially political correctness.

Venus in double Aquarius likes a freedom that is perhaps more extreme than the Sagittarian urge; Aquarius freedom is lighter, not quite so desperate on the outside as mental attitudes are what count. They can sense the first chill in a relationship when their freedom is called in to question, and they expect total trust; they do not expect to have to explain themselves. The new Aquarian nature coupled with the old Aquarian nature is happy to explore different types of relationship.

The fighting energy of Mars is keen to establish new boundaries, with others, with systems and with ideas. They see the inner attitudes as the precursor to outer change and they are happy to change their own actions for a better life; keeping an ear open for cracks in the systems they are quick to change the way they do things. They see exciting new prospects in many situations and are impatient with people who hold back progress. Though they relish excitement and new big events with many people, they also like a calm environment where they can pursue lines of thoughts, projects or just read.

Of course the freedom spun by the stars of Aquarius suit Jupiter; Aquarius urges Jupiter to think outside the box, believe in those ideals and imagine an even better world. And Jupiter is first out the box. There is no end to the wonder these people find in the world and in each other. They are intellectually aroused by other cultures and use every opportunity to make their own lifestyle more interesting; there is so much for them to learn about and use to make their own lives more original; evolution, genetics, cyber technologies, space travel, weather, volcanoes, aliens and animals.

New situations, systems, parameters and rules are the domain of Saturn and here they are honoured and maintained and restructured as this ruling Saturn sees fit. There is a strong sense of independent responsibility that they can see the way forward. As a new world-order establishes itself Saturn has a sharp eye for where the new hasn't worked or where the old is obsolete. They can be equally cynical about modern times and traditional methods; they play the Devil's advocate to leave no stone unturned in finding the best, possibly unthought-of solution.

OLD PISCES/NEW AQUARIUS

Old Water – New Air

The mystic uses astrology casting horoscopes under sharp, halogen light.

The Piscean nature of going with the flow and dreaminess as well as compassion for all beings are the ones held as typically Piscean and reveal they are part of the bible of protected traits. Going with the flow forever is aimless; a time comes when a choice will be made. The choice reveals that nothing can go on aimlessly for ever. Commitments must be made and those commitments are made for the benefit of all people. Dreaminess cannot go on either with no waking point. The waking point is excitement; a real idea or a brilliant inspiration that needs to be followed through. And compassion also is a trait that has a tipping point. After so much compassion you cannot but help want to make the world a better place; you cannot but help define the concerns of others. In defining the concerns for others you are one step closer to making the world a better place. The motivations of New Aquarius are rooted in the oneness of Pisces.

These are the Pisces from the Tropical zodiac who are not particularly fussed with other people's feelings compared to other people's rights. They are more likely to join a group or do something that helps underdogs have their share of social money or healthcare. They are concerned that poorer and less able people should have the same as richer more capable people; they believe in the equality of individuals. They have an innate emotional understanding and a good way of gaining intellectual rapport and so they do well as counsellors; they watch, listen and feel for what the situation demands of them. This concoction of starry influence is very motivated to help others who are worse off than themselves and they often get emotionally involved too. If it weren't for people like these Ascendants, those that are trapped between red tape and laws would get ignored. These are the action medics for the soul; balancing Water and Air to keep their heads above Water. They have an ability to get to the crucial point of what aid is needed with their unstinting desire to help, to listen and to understand. Often these Ascendants have a lifestyle choc-a-bloc with appointments, dates and plans and just fill their lives up further and forget to take on board things to do for themselves. They are comfortable in busy situations; as if their souls know they are here to help, and they use every incident to experience what they can about somebody else's life. They may seek out hardship deliberately to experience how other people survive.

It is good to see the effect of the Sidereal constellations breaking through the ways of the Tropical zodiac and I think here Old Pisces is starting to grow out of Old Pisces; they are no longer hooked on being blissed out; they want to be more useful. They can see the end and are part of the beginning; their new sense of destiny calls them to take part in the modern world and do their thing. Perhaps the stars of Aquarius have created a taste for contemporary life; for the technologies and the possibilities of sharing and readjusting balances. But it is hard work doing the work that is not fully valued. They try to shake off their old cloak and swing their arms in time to the music but there's an odd feeling that they are one of a kind and on the verge of something strange and new; they just don't feel like they fully fit in – it is this very feeling that inspires them to help others find where they belong. This Sun is sensitive to the sense of not belonging, in others. They can see it in others because they have known it in themselves and their mission is to help everyone to find their place. This solar nature is socially very flexible and welcome in many circles because they can tune in to the ideals and underlying pathos of a group. Also music and cutting edge music is their thing. All Pisces have a musical ear because they are quiet inside; they watch the world and listen to their own inner response, making them comfortable with meditations too. They can hear the bell, see the signs and are capable of following their own inner visions. Aquarius puts icing on the cake for living in the modern world; for now the original thinkers and the drummers who beat to their own drum can find many expressions in modern society.

New Aquarius encourages the old Pisces Moon to sit up and look around; there are many more impressions to deal with in a new way. Old Pisces' solution was to go with the flow and let everything take its course; it was safe enough to do that because these gentle Moons had a childhood that taught them to trust. The old wise karmic souls know all too well the disappointments the world can bring and so Aquarius helps to stand back a little; not take things quite so personally; these Moons can be sage-like for the closest people to them. They do not pretend to be able to save the world or make huge sacrifices of themselves, it is enough they keep their head above Water, keep their wits about them and make the days as sweet as possible; for who knows how long anything lasts. They carry the feeling of being an alien in a vast universe and their awareness of tragedy, poetry, love and all the grand movements of the soul makes this Moon sit above the Earth watching and aching with sympathy.

Mercury in this position makes people who are good at conversation; people who make nice company; everyone's friend. They listen and pick up on the feelings behind the words; they understand the threads in the stories and reply with gentle originality. When they speak each word is meant; they are not the kind of people who say something because they ought, they say what they say because it is what they want known. They can inject the most boring conversation with interest and meaning while still keeping it calm. They mosey from one subject to another, trying to understand all the different viewpoints while maintaining their own; they make good dancers who don't lose the beat.

The Venus nature of Old Pisces radiates a magnetic love for everyone. They feel love and respect for humanity and animals; their magnetic appeal is approachable and attracts gentleness while Aquarius wants them to live this vibe more deeply. It is seen in soldiers to animal rights activists; their idealism is so deeply moving they feel compelled to love, protect and honour on a large scale. They love being part of something larger than themselves and they find themselves by losing themselves. Exaltation and idealization rule this spirit.

Where Venus of this sector is influenced to join with others to help animals or some other cause, Mars here is keen to go out and fight for the cause. I have always been surprised by the many Tropical Pisces Mars who go into the army. I am sure it is because of the cause, of helping the weak; it is huge and national so it can be all encompassing and there is a sense of sacrifice that makes this route appealing for them. To Pisces – Aquarius sacrifice is a value not a loss. They are going into the army to save us from war; not to go to war. The idealism of this Pisces/Aquarius Mars breaks my heart open to this nature. They fight for a cause way bigger than themselves and become more than just one lone person. These are the activists, the travellers and the artists forcing us to accept the oddballs and misfits. Whatever this Mars choses to do is because there is deep passion in their bones; sacrificing their individuality to help those that are smaller.

The higher mind is taken up with wanting to make the world a better place to live. They see the causes of things and want to add something to alter the balance for animals and people less fortunate than themselves. These Pisces are optimistic and lucky; they have such big dreams even a little luck takes them further on to the road of success. They see many opportunities to make a point or bring some aid. These people live through imagination and so their aim is to provide for their body the wonderful things that they can imagine; successfully manifesting their vision they in turn give generously to others.

I heard it said once that Saturn here tends to feel sorry for themselves; it is almost opposite to Jupiter in this position. Without the optimism and the sense of luck, the reality hits home; though Saturn here probably tries harder and for longer to achieve the same things and once it has achieved them, holds its successes closer. There is sadness with this position that the native is always aware of just what has being sacrificed; which can never be equal to the material gain. The loss of time and effort, which could be spent relaxing with people they love is a double bind to them because without the effort they wouldn't have the lifestyle they wanted.

OLD PISCES/NEW PISCES

Old Water – New Water

Someone plumbed a tap to syphon the free table Water; someone left it running, someone might never turn it off.

There are some Ascendants who are said to live in the past; who come home from a hard day's work and drift off, sleeping idly, daydreaming about events and linking it all up with what else they have known. When someone said Pisces was the dustbin of zodiac, they meant just these few degrees where the native soaks everything in. They are unbelievably laid back about going out into the world to do something; not out of laziness, but like the Taoist priests, who believe that by doing less the world would be better off without interference. The double dose of Water show these natives feel and imagine their way through life. It is how they face the world.

The old meets the new past; from this position in the sky the stars bestow intuitive and psychic awareness. Despite their natural tendency to sink into the past these Suns have a talent for recognizing patterns which they can link to past experience and predict future events. When under-developed these Suns can be plagued with strange forebodings yet still do not feel urged to meddle in the affairs of the world. They flow along with the tides of life like the perfect Taoist student, they are the modern mystics but strangely they are the last to see that. Often they can reject their own inner-knowing as stupid because our modern civilization does not fully appreciate such delicate living. This is a Tropical Sun who knows they are Pisces. Old Pisces/New Pisces, they know they are Pisces, whereas the earlier born Tropical Pisces Suns knew there was something else there as well. The Sidereal stars of Pisces/Pisces are crossing the boundary of the Point of the Vernal Equinox and these stars cross boundaries. They merge the edges. Just as the past is merged into the future, the boundaries between people and cultures are softened. These Suns are more than aware that the status, sex or nationality of a person does not separate our souls. When these stars have finally swam across the Vernal Point of Spring then mystic and intuitive awareness will also be recognized as part of humanities' make-up. When these stars have moved over the vernal equinox the boundaries of countries may have dissolved.

These are the ultra-compassionate Moons: picking up on everybody else's vibes and getting all stirred up inside about injustices and why someone said something a certain way; but they are not thinking per-se; they are watching all the feelings swooshing in their belly and adding different faces to different swooshy feelings; that's how they know things inside. They excel in ambience in the home; laying tables for after school tea, a dinner for two, ladies from the W.I or a raucous bash with their friends; each situation is treated imaginatively to create effect. The Pisces/Pisces Moon parents may seem indulgent to the more practical Moons but children learn from their parents what there is to value and these imaginative Moons show us the depth and importance of ambience for a great quality of life.

Imagination rules again with story-telling as a favourite way of understanding the world. Mercury helps us think and make sense of ourselves in relation to the world and here Mercury works in parables and similes, poetry and fables. This is a cine camera mind rather than the snap shot mind or a panoramic view; the scene is kept running, it runs into the next frame, everything is related into an alchemy of words or numbers or music. Whichever media the Pisces/Pisces mind is disciplined in, the boundaries blur.

All loving Venus blisses out here, she loves everyone. There is a strong feeling of feeling beautiful and loveable and tender. That is why this Venus could not bring itself to fight; it is so tender and they treat others with the same tenderness, there isn't a bone in their body that wants to fight. They would rather hide or retreat than be part of combat and this nature is a strong part of their psychological make-up if they have Venus in this position. They are so sensitive and open in a happy place all the good feelings get soaked up and in response every molecule of their being vibrates with a calming and loving rhythm - the feeling surrounds them and spreads like a wave throughout the room. If this Venus belongs in the nativity of someone who is unkind then the native literally switches from unkind to kind; so strong is this position of Venus, it cannot be integrated to be anything other than its own blissful vibration.

As with all influences of Pisces, on Mars there is an acceptance of sacrifice. Sacrifice to make them stronger. They can fight to the death; this is no weak Mars. But it has to have something it wants to fight for, something that is worth dying for, so this Mars is marked by its strong passion for what it stands up for. A sacrifice could be time, money, space and that is why so many Pisces/Pisces are known for music as music takes practice and practice means to sacrifice time spent on other things. These Mars are passionate too but where Scorpio – Tropical and Sidereal are defensive, Tropical and Sidereal Pisces Mars are defenceless. The addictive nature of Mars here is because they can give and give for the goal they so believe in that if the goal begins to recede they can still sacrifice, as if the sacrifice itself would bring the goal. This is why the principles of Virgo and Pisces complement each other; Virgo monitors and Pisces gives its all.

Pisces frees Jupiter with imagination and the higher mind finds correspondence with intuition. There is a strong sense of self belief with this placement, because its limitations seem so far away. It has perfect faith and easily hooks into a story and the wonderful feeling of a happy ending. Here is the mystical philosopher enthusiastically searching by letting go, to understand something that is incomprehensible with the ordinary mind.

Saturn, right at the end sees the end. The past has gone; no wonder this placement can get depressed. It has the capacity to work for something bigger which would be its saviour but it doesn't have the belief and faith which Jupiter does. There can be disappointment and cynicism which can be alleviated by work and the sacrificing of time; which in true Saturn style - it sacrifices time to make more time. This is a wise Saturn that uses stoicism to understand the disappointments in life.

TRANSMUTATION OF THE ELEMENTS

Earth becomes Fire: what is solid and known, proven and routine becomes belief and inspiration with opportunity to climb higher.

Water becomes Air: what is felt, emoted and imagined becomes the urge to use communication to connect.

Fire becomes Water: what inspires and whets appetites becomes passion to share.

Air becomes Earth: ideas become manifest; abstract art, representations and reflections express multiple views.

Isn't the transmutation of the elements a miraculous thing?

APPENDIX

ASTRONOMY OF THE PRECESSION OF THE EQUINOXES

There is only one zodiac. The zodiac is an *imaginary* ring around the Earth, which the Sun, Moon, planets and the asteroids that circle the Sun all seem to travel. From Earth it appears that the Moon and all the planets circle the Earth; it also looks like the Sun circles the Earth in this ring too. This ring is the zodiac.

The zodiac ring is studded by stars. It is like a wheel with the stars painted on it. The stars don't move (except for the proper motion of stars – which is extraordinarily slow - and the 26000 year cycle of the Precession of the Equinoxes which is somewhat 'faster' and explained below). The stars don't move but the ring from our perspective appears to turn.

The ring appears to turn but it is the Earth that turns, as you know; eastward.

The stars that are painted on the zodiac wheel are always the same stars; these are the stars of the zodiac signs Aries, Taurus and so on. Some people include Ophiucus in the zodiac (in my opinion – off with his head![4])

The borders for each of these constellations were given precise co-ordinates in 1930 by the International Astronomy Union. Before then the days of the year marked their 30° boundaries. Theoretically every 365¼ days the Sun should be in the same position against the zodiac of painted stars. However, it is not. The reason that the Sun is not at the exact same position on a yearly basis is because of Precession of the Equinoxes and Precession of the Equinoxes is the reason we refer to a Tropical or a Sidereal zodiac.

---

[4] The stars of Ophiucus have always been sneaking up behind Sagittarius and Scorpio, trying to butt in between them; so there is no need to include these stars. And anyways, as Ptolemy said, "we cannot be certain of how much of an influence stars have from the same degree of arc."(Tetrabiblos Part 1)

Precession of the Equinoxes happens because the Earth's axis wobbles; it traces an imaginary circle. The Earth spins more like a gyroscope slowing down than a perfect spinner. This means that the Earth's axis does not stay fixed, it does not point in the same direction all the time. If a line was drawn through the Earth, through the north and south geographic poles and extended into the sky, then the extended axis (north and south) would trace a circle over 26,000 years. (approx.) The Precession of the Equinoxes is a 26,000 year cycle that reveals itself by shifting Earth's alignment of the Spring Equinox by 1° every 72 years; every 72 years the Sun rises 1° more *before* 0° Aries; accumulating over 25,686 years through the full 360°.

Spring Equinox is always around the day we call 21st March. At this time of the year the Earth and the Sun align perpendicularly giving the impression of equal night and day everywhere on Earth. At the time of the Spring Equinox the Sun appears to be in front of the stars of 0° ♈ - well it used to – now the ring with the constellations painted on it has shifted. The day when the Sun sits in front of 0° ♈ is now about 15th April; but the day 21st March is the day the Sun and Earth align perpendicularly for the Equinox to happen. On 21st March, in the Sidereal zodiac we see 6°♓. The Sun appears to move forward every day through the zodiac; 6°, 7°, 8° Pisces from 21st March and at the same time the Sun appears to move back 1° every 72 years. The Sun's 'movement' is apparent because of what we see from Earth is only our perception. But it IS our perception that matters.

The **Tropical zodiac** is a map of the ecliptic belt aligning 0° Aries to the Spring Equinox. This means that on the 21st March every year 0° Aries should be exactly on the dawn horizon, with the Sun. But as we have seen the stars change position over a long period of time and 0° Aries is no longer where it should be. The Tropical zodiac is therefore a theoretical zodiac. However; the meaning of the constellations are in tune with the cultures of the times, the seasons and the socio-economic ways for many people. For instance; Leos are born the youngest in their school years and in the height of the summer. Their birthday parties are looked forward to and celebrated by their peers as the long summer holidays mean many children see less friends during the summer holidays. Conversely, Virgo babies are the eldest in their year. They are encouraged to look after and be mindful of their younger classmates. How Virgoan it is to serve. Look at Sagittarius with Christmas coming up and Capricorn to maintain the structure of the tradition. So the Tropical zodiac still serves us; as if the archetypes of the season are embedded in our culture.

The **Sidereal zodiac** began as the Tropical zodiac but 1° was deducted every 72 years from 0° Aries. The Sidereal zodiac is also a theoretical zodiac but the constellations are aligned with the Spring Equinox at 6° (or 8°) Pisces and then each of the 12 constellations are allocated 30° degrees. The 24° that are used to adjust the Tropical zodiac to the Sidereal zodiac is a number that has accumulated for 24 x 72 = 1728 years. This accumulating number is called the **Ayanamsa**. The Ayanamsa is used in Indian astrology and different astrologers use different Ayanamsas. There is debate as to what year the first degree was subtracted. I use an Ayanamsa of 24°.[5] I have decided upon 24° as this aligns well enough with the Astronomical zodiac and is also used by most Indian astrologers[6].

The **Astronomical zodiac** is a replication of the actual lengths of each constellation in the zodiac. As agreed by the IAU, the boundaries for each of the zodiac constellations are various;

---

[5] An Ayanamsa of 24° points to the time of the First Ecumenical Council of Nicea in 325 AD (within the 72 years for 1°.

[6] The Ayanamsa is often calculated to precision with minutes as it shows the time ticking through 72 years and is relevant for natal charts.

some are more and some are less than 30°[7]. However astrologers only need the 30° for each constellation and the constellations themselves may only have been markers in the sky which explains their higgledy-piggledy shapes. For instance, some of the stars in the constellations cross over the stars of the adjacent constellation. And some of the stars of the constellations don't even reach the 30° marker. It could be that the ancients had a simple knowledge of the stars that went something like, 'you see those 3 stars of Pisces forming a point? Well don't look at the point, look at the line of the 2 stars making that point, follow that line up to the faint star of the tail of the Ram of Aries; and there is the boundary between Pisces and Aries; conjecture I know…

WHY FISHTAIL?

Sidereal and Tropical zodiacs both allocate 30° for each sign.

Pisces, the sign of the fishes, is still on the Ascendant at the Spring Equinox. There is still 6° of Pisces left for this Age. This means there are still approximately 430 years left of the Age of Pisces, according to Sidereal astrology.

However, **astronomically**, each of the other 3 angles – the Midheaven, the I.C and the Descendant – has each been crossed by their preceeding sign within the last 72 years. This is because the constellations are of varying length and Pisces is a sign of long ascension. It is significant that the other 3 angles of the world (the summer solstice, the winter solstice, the autumn equinox and the spring equinox are the 4 angles of the world) have each changed signs – recently! – within 72 years.

Also, on February 4th and 5th 1962, Sun, Moon, Mercury, Venus, Mars, Jupiter, Saturn and South node were all in Tropical Aquarius, Sidereal Capricorn. Astrologically this was a

---

[7] In my book, Age of the Fishtail, I have mapped and discuss the Astronomical zodiac in relation to the Tropical zodiac.

significant event, though typically, astronomers and critics do not assign any world change to this time. Instead, as in all astrological workings, the change is part of a process; and I think we will all agree that significant changes to humanity across the globe has been in effect these last 50 plus years.

Significant change in astrological terms is when an individual and individuals affect a tipping point. People who had a Planet or angle aspected on 4th/5th February 1962 would have had an opportunity to make a significant change in their life, or even to have nurtured a profound idea born of inspiration. Many other people would have been affected by opposition, trines or squares; not quite as strong and not necessarily smooth either. Some people could have ignored the cosmic prodding. Some adults could have nurtured their children with the new awareness and children will have grown with an innate understanding of a new awareness which in turn they would grow up with, act out and pass on; thereby eventually reaching a tipping point of change.

As an aside; 3 years previously to all the Planets in Aquarius, in 1959, the Dalai Lama left Tibet for a safe place in India. Alan Watts, Ram Das, Aldous Huxley are a few of the interesting, materially astute and articulate seekers of truth that were prominent at that time – 1962. The New age movement officially began in the 1970's.

The next time all the visible Planets, Sun and Moon are in the same constellation is in a few hundred years. According to the Swiss Ephemeris on 25th November 2516 all the visible Planets will be in Sagittarius. On 10th December 2009 Lahiri Ayanamsa was exactly 24°; that is near enough the year 2010. Add 432 years – which is 72 years for each 1° x 6 for each degree that has yet to be precessed and we get 2442. The year 2516 is just 74 years more than the predicted 432 more years till the end of the Age of Pisces and 74 years is just 2 more years than the next 1° of precession.

Looking at the Ages by degrees it seems we can say within 72 years when a new Age will begin and the old one ends. But the work of the Distinctions and the nth degree shows us a process that flows into each other; just like the caterpillar is goo for a period of time in its cocoon and the defining point of transmutation is when the butterfly completely climbs out of its cocoon. Maybe the year 2516 – 74 years after the 'end' of Pisces is a good enough time to define the emergence of the Age of Aquarius. However, all the Planets in Aquarius did not signify the end of an Age in 1962 though it was a marker of significant times. Ages may best be interpreted as a ticking process that ticks with the average human lifespan.

So although we are still in the Age of Pisces, it is the tail end. Yet without a doubt we are in the midst of momentous change in consciousness. Never before have we, the masses, known we have individual destinies and meaningful lives influenced by the heavens. In previous times only kings, queens, emperors, empresses and other people exalted by birth were considered to be worthy of cosmic influence. That is why the tail end of the Age of Pisces is given a specific name; Age of the Fishtail.

Also published by Fishtail Arts & Astrology:

Cosmic Journal 2018 (also in hardback)

Just Cosmic 2018

Astro Journal 2018

7

www.ingramcontent.com/pod-product-compliance
Lightning Source LLC
Chambersburg PA
CBHW051254110526
44588CB00026B/2985